1998

POLITICAL CARTOONS
IN THE MIDDLE EAST

POLITICAL CARTOONS
IN THE MIDDLE EAST

Fatma Müge Göçek, ed.

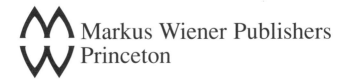 Markus Wiener Publishers
Princeton

Reprinted from *Princeton Papers: Interdisciplinary Journal of
Middle Eastern Studies,* Volume VI.

For information write to: Markus Wiener Publishers
231 Nassau Street, Princeton, NJ 08542

Library of Congress Cataloging-in-Publication Data

Political cartoons in the Middle East/
 Fatma Müge Göçek, ed.
  Includes bibliographical references
  ISBN 1-55876-156-X (hc)
  ISBN 1-55876-157-8 (pb)
  1. Turkey—Politics and government—1905—Caricatures and cartoons.
 2. Iran—History—1905–1911—Caricatures and cartoons.
 3. Persian Gulf War, 1991—Tunisia—Caricatures and cartoons.
 4. Women—Turkey—Caricatures and cartoons.
 5. Political cartoons.   I. Göçek, Fatma Müge.
 DS44.P65   1997
 956.04'02'07—dc21   97-34020
                                                                      CIP

Printed in the United States of America on acid-free paper.

Contents

Political Cartoons as a Site of Representation and Resistance in the Middle East

FATMA MÜGE GÖÇEK

When Necmeddin Erbakan, the first Islamist prime minister of Turkey, wanted to suppress the widespread rumors about an impending military coup in July 1997, he ordered an inquiry into the allegedly seditious activities of a group of ten intellectuals: prominent among them was one political cartoonist, Salih Memecan. Similarly in Egypt, the Egyptian government often expressed ire over the political cartoons of Ahmed Hijazi; the Syrian government's discomfort with such cartoons led them to silence cartoonists by disabling them to publish in any media other than the state-controlled one. Why do political cartoons in the Middle East form such a formidable threat? This article argues that it is the potential of political cartoons to generate change—by freeing the imagination, challenging the intellect, and resisting state control—that produces such a reaction. Political cartoons also provide a rare public glimpse into the thoughts and opinions of the people in the Middle East, especially to those living in societies dominated by the state.

This article approaches the question of why political cartoons are a significant social force in the Middle East through an analysis of the historical emergence of political cartoons. It first investigates the multiple attributes of a political cartoon and identifies its unique capacity to simultaneously represent ideas and resist control as the most significant characteristic. The analysis of the emergence of political cartoons in Europe demonstrates how this unique capacity developed as the opinions of the people contested the interests of the state through cartoons. The subsequent study of the Middle Eastern adoption of cartoons in turn identifies how people incorporated local forms and meanings into this Western product to make it their own, thus transforming its sites of representation and resistance into their own social realities.

Political Cartoons as a Site of Representation and Resistance

The political cartoon has emerged as a very significant social medium because of the multiplicity of meanings and forms embedded within: it contains both a visual and a textual message on political events presented through cultural symbols as interpreted by the caricaturist. The immense social impact of the political cartoon derives from its simultaneous appeal to the intellect, conscience, and emotion: the cartoon presents a picture as the essence of truth, a message as to what ought to be done on behalf of the deserving, and a mood created through artistic technique and allegorical imagery of how the viewer ought to feel over what is happening (Press 1981: 62). It represents the cartoonist's interpretation of larger societal practices and forces through the use of textual and visual codes (Chaplin 1994: 1). The process of decoding the cartoon introduces more layers of meaning as multiple audiences find in it their own rendition of the world around them (Hall 1984; Strinati 1995: 127). This rich representation is also able to resist control because of the ambiguities in the message that result from the multiple levels of meaning.

In analyzing domination and the arts of resistance, James Scott (1990: xii) identifies the humor embedded in cartoons as "a hidden transcript that represents a critique of power spoken behind the back of the dominant." Political cartoons acquire this capacity to dismantle the public transcript by transposing the event from the realm of serious events to that of fiction, visually distorting the subject, and then presenting it all to the reader in the form of a puzzle to be decoded (Mulkay 1988: 202). They transform everything into "cheerfully irreverent quotation marks" (Bakhtin in Goldstein 1990: 16), criticizing, undermining, challenging, and devaluing categories and events that appear natural. Especially in societies where people do not feel free to speak openly, cartoons with their ambiguous and hidden meanings enable them to communicate to one another both their frustrations and their desires (Marsot 1980; Townsend 1992; Rodrigues and Collinson 1995). These ambiguities also help protect the cartoonists in their attacks, and, at the same time, enable readers that keep thinking about it to start to delve into latent meanings embedded in them, thereby expanding the impact of the message (Schutz 1995: 51–52; Morris 1991: 228). The history of political cartoons reveals the social processes through which these characteristics of representation and resistance were created.

The Emergence of Political Cartoons in Europe

The precursors of political cartoons were the Renaissance broadsheets, topical and political images printed on loose sheets of paper to be sold to the public (Sheppard 1994: 36). These images were often drawn from an emblem book that developed a pictorial language from the medieval conventions of allegory and myth. Metaphors of dark and light, for instance, were employed to allegorically present a moral truth, often accompanied by a motto and a text in verse; ad hoc symbols constructed for a specific use (Sheppard 1994: 40). One such book, Cesare Ripa's *Iconologia*, which was published in Rome in 1593, described personified virtues, vices, emotions, and other abstract concepts; with the appearance of subsequent editions and translations in French, German, Dutch, English, and Spanish, sets of shared images became consolidated throughout Europe (Sheppard 1994: 37–38). A significant feature of these images was the drawing of humans as animals, a skill developed by G. B. Della Porta in sixteenth century Rome. During the same time period, such images of fellow citizens turned out in abundance by Annibale and Agostino Caracci led to the formulation of the word *caricatura* (Press 1981: 33). It is noteworthy that the emergence of the medium of caricature corresponded to a period in European history when human-inspired forms of representation had started to gradually replace the spiritual ones.

The medium of the caricature, thus pioneered during the Italian Renaissance, became especially popular in seventeenth century France in articulating the opposition to the crown; it gave political dissidents the chance both to delegitimate the king through ridicule and to generate a new shared set of political symbols. The success of caricatures in illuminating the emerging "revolutionary character" (Boime 1992: 256) led the French king Louis XIV to ban this medium. The caricaturists resisted the ban by going to Holland to publish their work (Maurice and Cooper 1970: 9). The Dutch Republic, which was much more open to forms of political expression, developed a brisk print trade, including an underground traffic of caricatures into France. In the late eighteenth century, these widely circulating political cartoons certainly hastened the French Revolution by constantly deriding the French king and his court and by venerating new Republican symbols such the *citoyen*. The frequent references to the citizens of Greece and Rome further legitimated the message by enabling it to capture "a slice of eternity" (Mosse 1985: 15).

Print runs that had reached the capacity of fifty thousand copies in eighteenth century[1] England (Porter 1988: 190) escalated to hundreds of thousands in the 1850s when the steam-powered press made its way to the printing houses; as the print media became more and more accessible to all the citizens of the French Republic, the cartoons reached even a larger audience through their accessibility to the illiterate. Also the improving print techniques, especially photoengraving, which became possible in the 1880s, gave much more freedom of expression to the artist in his interpretations (Sheppard 1994: 36–37).

These increasing production capacities in the nineteenth and twentieth centuries were accompanied by changing political priorities that further enhanced the social significance of political cartoons. The term *cartoon* itself made its appearance in 1843 when the British magazine *Punch* "parodied the inept proposals submitted for the new Houses of Parliament frescoes" (Sheppard 1994: 39). This expression of public aesthetic opinion was part of a larger transformation into nation-states. The newly emerging public opinion and the imagined community of the nation made prodigious use of the political cartoon as an accessible form of visual rhetoric. This medium became especially crucial in mobilizing civilians to fight for newly emerging nations as governments used political cartoons to trivialize the enemy and embellish allies.

During World War I, the first instance of total war, cartoons became a significant means of propagandawith which "to beat the enemy not only on the military front, but to demoralize his population" (Demm 1993: 163). Political cartoons were employed on both fronts: at home, they were used to mobilize the population both morally and intellectually for the war, explain setbacks, confirm belief in the superiority of the fatherland, and proclaim the hope of final victory; against the enemy, political cartoons were utilized to put the population in dismay through ridiculing them, and constantly displaying their ineptitude, cowardice, and effeminacy. A "visual warfare" thus paralleled the one being fought at the frontier (Kleeblatt 1993; Weisberg 1987). Germany was the first major power to recognize the significance of political cartoons as a medium of warfare and to actively finance humor magazines. The opportunity to orchestrate public opinion through print and visual media then led to the emergence of propaganda as a pivotal war department.

The increasing significance of cartoons also meant, however, an escalation in political control through censorship. With censorship, political cartoons started to transform from a site of representation of ideas and values to one of resistance against state control; new meanings and symbol systems emerged to criticize the authorities. The French caricaturist Charles Philipon criticized the French king Louis-Philippe (1830–1848) by playing upon the multiple connotations of *la poire*, the pear, especially its meaning of "fathead" in slang, to depict the king as a pear. Even though the king immediately sentenced him to prison, this action made the caricaturist and his caricature even more popular and permanently conferred upon the pear a new political meaning. Governor Pennypacker of Pennsylvania employed another control against his negative portrayal in cartoons: he outlawed in 1903 visual depictions of persons as animals. Yet his measure led to the use of vegetables instead, demonstrating the resiliency of the resistance to state control (Sheppard 1994: 26–27). In the same era, even censorship itself could not escape the ridicule of cartoonists who started to depict it as a stern, humorless woman with a vast pair of scissors in hand.

Censorship escalated in particular during wartime when people closed ranks and governments became less tolerant of criticism. During World War I, in the German editorial offices of satirical journals, many cartoonists "put their talents at the service of the nation" (Coupe 1992:

24), voluntarily restricting their freedom of interpretation. Yet additional control was also imposed by the German government, which controlled the paper and print supplies of the print media, ordering them to follow the official line and to subject themselves to censorship by local military commanders in return for receiving these supplies. For instance, the propaganda office in Berlin gave the editor of the humor magazine *Phosphor* quality paper for printing the magazine in return for "fighting against all Bolshevist, Communist, and Spartacist ideas by means of satire" (Simmons 1993: 47). During World War II, all major military powers had propaganda offices that recognized and employed political cartoons to influence public opinion.

In late twentieth century Europe, the increasing intervention of the nation-state into the lives of its citizens and the surfacing social divides based on race, gender, and class further enhanced the significance of political cartoons as a site of resistance. Political cartoons also did not remain a medium particular to Europe; they accompanied Europe's gradual technological, economic, and political domination over the rest of the world. The non-Western world including the Middle East promptly started to employ this medium to scorn their own Westernizing selves and to ridicule and delegitimate their Western rulers. Local myths, folktales, and aesthetic forms were quickly synthesized into these new interpretations, first to symbolically authenticate the burgeoning nationalist movements and then to resist them.

The Development of Political Cartoons in the Middle East

The appearance of cartoons in the Middle East during the mid-nineteenth century coincided with the rise of Western influence. The first Ottoman cartoon materialized in the journal *İstanbul* in 1867, approximately thirty-five years after the publication of the first Ottoman official gazette, *Takvim-i Vekayi* (Chronicle of Events), and fifteen years after the publication of the first humor gazette[2] by an Ottoman Armenian, Hovsep Vartanyan (Çeviker 1986: 17). In Egypt, Ya'qub Sannu published in 1887 *Al-Tankit wa Al-Tabkit* (Joking and Censure), a humorous newspaper criticizing the West; he also drew the first cartoon in the Arab press. Other journals soon appeared, although the Egyptian press remained the major source of print for cartoons in the Arab world until 1925, when Michael Tays established the humor newspaper *Kannas al-Shawari* (The Road Sweeper) in Iraq. Other pioneering cartoonists include Khalid Kahhala who began publishing the satirical gazette *Al Mudhik al-Mubki* (The Weeping Joker) in Syria in 1929 and Bayram al-Tunisi whose *al-Shabab* (Youth) emerged in Tunisia in 1932 (Kishtainy 1985: 73, 94, 97).

How did the political cartoons in the Middle East interpret this Western form? Even though some, including Frantz Fanon, have construed cartoons as primary agents of Western cultural imperialism and alienation, recent scholarship (Douglas and Douglas 1994, Abu-Lughod 1989, Mitchell 1989) has advanced a more textured analysis arguing that the adoption process was much more interactive in nature. Cartoons, they have argued, have become a site of negotiation often "borrowing, mixing, and inventing forms" from both Western and indigenous contexts (Abu-Lughod 1989: 7). There were indeed many local forms and meaning structures that contributed to the transformation of the medium. The pre-existing sources of humor deriving from intentional linguistic blunders, misapplications of the holy scripture, and reinterpretations of historical incidents were immediately added to the repertoire of political cartoons. Popular shadow plays and the heavily illustrated texts reformed the aesthetic and visual foundation of cartoons, as did the orally transmitted humor ridiculing despotic authority, especially the tales of Juha or Nasreddin Hoca, the wise fool (Kishtainy 1985: 37, 62). The end-product was a hybrid form that was able to trasform the Western product into "its own native pictures, balloons and heroes" (Douglas and Douglas 1994: 9). For instance, an Ottoman political cartoon often adopted the Western symbol of liberty in its image, but then presented it within the traditional form and aesthetic[3] of Ottoman popular culture as a conversation between the shadow play characters Karagöz and Hacivat.

This hybridity generated an additional layer of ambiguity often enabling cartoon drawings to challenge the dominant "official images" of both the West and the local government (Slyomovics 1992; 1993). As Tim Mitchell (1989) notes, however, this local empowerment through the reinterpretation of political cartoons has generated success in winning a few battles but certainly not the war; the economic, political, and technological dominance of the West still continues unabated. Even though cartoons in the Middle East interpret Western images with a local twist, and thus partially subvert the embedded Western images and values, they fail to alter the existing Western forms of domination.

The emergence of this unique medium was closely followed, as in Europe, by the development of censorship clauses and laws (Çeviker 1986: 61). In the Ottoman Empire, even though ninety-two satire newpapers sprang up during the year of Sultan Abdülhamid's dethronement, they could not escape the impact of a press law passed in 1909 and based on the French one which limited freedom of the press. Most of these satirical gazettes were censored first by the Ottoman military government during World War I and then by the Allied Powers that occupied Constantinople until the end of the Turkish War of Independence (Çeviker 1988: 17, 50, 61–64). During this period, Ottoman caricaturists tried to resist censorship by many creative measures—for instance, some sent erasable drawings for approval that they then replaced with their initial more politically provocative material (Çeviker 1991: 58–59). Others asked newspapers to leave the place of the censored cartoon a blank space, a common mode of resistance often employed in the Ottoman context as well as in many European[4] ones. Later, in both the successor nation-states of the Ottoman Empire and the Arab world, the advent of strong and despotic nation-states forced cartoonists to turn their weapons to against the local problems and indigenous politicians. As the "discrepancy between reality and conception" increased in the Arab world, Khalid Kishtainy (1985: 151) elucidates, political cartoons exploded as a medium of expression.

The essays in this collection explore the wide spectrum of political cartoons in the Middle East. Palmira Brummett from the University of Tennessee analyzes the images of women in Ottoman cartoon space, while Shiva Balaghi from the University of Vermont studies issues of nationalism in the caricatures from Qajar Iranian newspapers. Ayhan Akman from the University of Chicago concentrates on the issue of modernity in Turkish cartoons during the 1930–1975 period Mohamed-Salah Omri from Washington University at St. Louis takes up the issue of war and cartoons as he comments on the politicization of Tunisian cartoons during the Gulf War.

Notes

1. During the 1790s, hand coloring had also become standard practice (Godfrey 1984: 16).
2. The satirical gazettes in the Ottoman empire were published monthly, bi-monthly, weekly or daily, often by a well-educated class of men whose affairs included both literature and politics (Brummett, this volume; Çeviker 1988: 101).
3. The Ottoman adoption was similar to the Chinese one where it was argued that "to create a genuine national art, artists must attempt to adopt the Western use of perspective and of human anatomy into Chinese traditional ink-and-brush painting" (Hung 1994: 134).
4. The replacement of a forbidden caricature with a mostly blank page, often accompanied by a denunciation of the government's action and sometimes a detailed written description of the banned drawing was the most frequent technique of resistance employed in nineteenth century France; the other was the publication of the obviously mutilated caricature with blank spaces for the parts that were censored (Goldstein 1989: 15).

Bibliography

Abu-Lughod, Lila, 1989. "Bedouins, Cassettes and Technologies of Public Culture." *Middle East Report* 19/4: 7–11, 47.

Boime, Albert, 1992. "The Sketch and Caricature as Metaphors for the French Revolution." *Zeitschrift für Kunstgeschichte* 2: 256–67.

Boime, Albert, 1988. "Jacques-Louis David, Scatological Discourse in the French Revolution, and the Art of Caricature." *Arts Magazine* 62/6: 72–81.

Brummett, Palmira, 1995. *Image and Imperialism in the Ottoman Revolutionary Press*. Book Manuscript.

Çeviker, Turgut, 1991. *Gelişim Sürecinde Türk Karikatürü: Kurtuluş Savaşı Dönemi 1918–1923* (The Evolution of Turkish Caricature: the Period of the War of Independence (1918–1923)). İstanbul: Adam.

Çeviker, Turgut, 1988. *Gelişim Sürecinde Türk Karikatürü: Meşrutiyet Dönemi 1908–1918* (The Evolution of Turkish Caricature: the Constitutional Period (1908–1918)). İstanbul: Adam.

Çeviker, Turgut, 1986. *Gelişim Sürecinde Türk Karikatürü: Tanzimat Dönemi 1867–78 ve İstibdat Dönemi 1878–1908* (The Evolution of Turkish Caricature: the Reform (1867–78) and Autocracy (1878–1908) Periods). İstanbul: Adam.

Chaplin, Elizabeth, 1994. *Sociology and Visual Representation*. London: Routledge.

Coupe, William, 1992. "German Cartoons of the First World War." *History Today* 42: 23–31.

Crane, Diana, 1992. *The Production of Culture*. Newbury Park, Calif: Sage.

Demm, Eberhard, 1993. "Propaganda and Caricature in the First World War." *Journal of Contemporary History* 28: 163–92.

Douglas, Allen and F. Malti-Douglas, 1994.*Arab Comic Strips: Politics of an Emerging Mass Culture*. Bloomington, Ind.: Indiana University Press.

Fischer, Michael and Mehdi Abedi, 1990. *Debating Muslims: Cultural Dialogues in Postmodernity and Tradition*. Madison: University of Wisconsin Press.

Godfrey, Richard, 1984. *English Caricature 1620 to the Present*. London: Victoria and Albert Museum.

Goldstein, Judith, 1990. "An Innocent Abroad: How Mulla Daoud was lost and found in Lebanon, or the politics of ethnic theater in a nation of war." Pp. 15–31 in *National Ideologies and the Production of National Cultures*. American Ethnological Society Monograph Series No. 2.

Goldstein, Robert Justin, 1989. "The Debate over the Censorship of Caricature in Nineteenth-Century France." *Art Journal* 48/1: 9–15.

Hall, Stuart, 1984. "Encoding/decoding." Pp. 128–38 in *Culture, Media, Language: Working Papers in Cultural Studies*. Center for Contemporary Studies, University of Birmingham, England.

Hung, Chang-Tai, 1994. "The Fuming Image: Cartoons and Public Opinion in Late Republican China, 1945 to 1949." *Comparative Studies in Society and History* 36/1: 122–45.

Kishtainy, Khalid, 1985. *Arab Political Humor*. London: Quartet Books.

Kleeblatt, Norman L., 1993. "Merde! The Caricatural Attack against Emile Zola." *Art Journal* 52/3: 54–8.

Marsot, Afaf Lutfi al-Sayyid, 1980. "Humor: the Two-Edged Sword." *Middle Eastern Studies Bulletin* 14/1: 1–9.

Maurice, Arthur Bartlett and F. T. Cooper, 1970. *The History of Nineteenth Century in Caricature*. New York: Cooper Square Publishers.

Mitchell, Tim, 1989. "Culture Across Borders." *Middle East Report* 19/4: 4–6, 47.

Morris, Ray, 1991. "Cultural Analysis through Semiotics: Len Morris' Cartoons on Official Bilingualism." *Canad. Rev. Soc. and Anthro.* 28/2: 225–54.

Mosse, George L., 1985. *Nationalism and Sexuality: Respectability and Abnormal Sexuality in Modern Europe*. New York: Howard Fertig.

Mulkay, Michael, 1988. *On Humor: Its Nature and Its Place in Modern Society*. New York: Basil Blackwell.

Porter, Roy, 1988. "Seeing the Past." *Past and Present* 118: 186–205.

Press, Charles, 1981. *The Political Cartoon*. Rutherford, NJ: Fairleigh Dickinson University Press.

Rodrigues, Suzana B. and David L. Collinson, 1995. ""Having Fun?": Humor as Resistance in Brazil." *Organizational Studies* 16/5: 739–68.

Schutz, Charles, 1995. "Cryptic Humor: the subversive message of political jokes." *Humor* 8/1: 51–64.

Scott, James, 1990. *Domination and the Arts of Resistance: Hidden Transcripts*. New Haven: Yale University Press.

Sheppard, Alice, 1994. *Cartooning for Suffrage*. Albuquerque: University of New Mexico Press.

Simmons, Sherwin, 1993. "War, Revolution, and the Transformation of the German Humor Magazine, 1914–27." *Art Journal* 52/1: 46–54.

Slyomovics, Susan, 1993. "Cartoon Commentary: Algerian and Moroccan Caricatures from the Gulf War." *Middle East Report* 23/1: 21–4.

Slyomovics, Susan, 1992. "Algeria Caricatures the Gulf War." *Public Culture* 4/2: 93–9.

Strinati, Dominic, 1995. *An Introduction to Theories of Popular Culture*. London: Routledge.

Townsend, Mary Lee, 1992. *Forbidden Laughter: Popular Humor and the Limits of Repression in 19th–century Prussia*. Ann Arbor: University of Michigan Press.

Weisberg, Gabriel, 1987. "Propaganda as Art: The Dreyfus Affair as Popular Exhibition." *Arts Magazine* 62/4: 36–41.

Weisberg, Gabriel P., 1993. "In Deep Shit: The Coded Images of Travies in the July Monarchy." *Art Journal* 52/3: 36–40.

New Woman and Old Nag: Images of Women in the Ottoman Cartoon Space

PALMIRA BRUMMETT

In 1908, the Young Turk Revolution brought constitutional government to the Ottoman empire, a vast, traditional, and polyglot empire that managed to survive well into the modern era.[1] This revolution is notable for its freeing of the Ottoman press, long circumscribed and censored under the regime of the autocratic Sultan Abdülhamid. With censorship temporarily in abeyance, Ottoman literati, satirists, cartoonists, and social critics wielded their pens with great vigor, producing a striking florescence of the Istanbul press. The satirical press in this freewheeling era is significant for its representation of the concerns and anxieties of a society undergoing dramatic change. It framed the Ottoman situation in terms of a set of dichotomies: the old and the new, the Ottoman and the European, freedom and subordination, glory and dishonor. This essay proposes to examine some of the ways in which those dichotomies played themselves out in the Ottoman cartoon space of 1908–1911, focusing on the use of female imagery to suggest the paradoxes of empire. While the majority of cartoon figures were male, female figures played a set of highly significant roles in the satirical representation of revolutionary reality. They symbolized the nation, its honor, and its vulnerability; they were the centerpieces of satire on the threat of European cultural hegemony; they represented the poles of modernity and tradition.

Background to the Revolution

The revolution of July 1908 toppled Sultan Abdülhamid, effectively ending a thirty-two year reign and nearly five centuries of Ottoman monarchical rule in Istanbul.[2] Abdülhamid had been brought to power in 1876 by the fledgling Ottoman constitutionalists who deposed his predecessor and wrote for the empire a constitution based on a Belgian model. But constitutional government was not destined to become a nineteenth-century Ottoman phenomenon. Once the sultan had consolidated his power, he dissolved the newly installed Ottoman parliament after less than two years, banished and imprisoned his detractors, and established one of the most elaborate spy systems in the history of the monarchy. His reign, progressive in some areas, was considered synonymous with political repression and censorship of the press.

The constitutional movement, however, did not die; in 1908, under military pressure, Abdülhamid agreed to reinstate the constitution and a Chamber of Deputies was elected.[3] The new regime, in a very precarious position vis-a-vis the European powers, was immediately faced with serious challenges to the sovereignty of the Ottoman state. By the time Abdülhamid mounted the throne in 1876, the Ottoman empire had already surrendered much of its past glory, and some of its territory. The revolution in 1908 provided an opportunity for the Sublime Porte's enemies; Austria annexed Bosnia and Herzegovina and Bulgaria proclaimed its independence. Meanwhile, the empire was, for all practical purposes, bankrupt. The Ottoman Public Debt was established in 1881, under French direction, to administer the meeting of payments for the enormous Ottoman foreign debt. European trading partners benefited from favored nation trade status under a capitulatory regime which debilitated the economy of the once prosperous Ottoman state. European and some American entrepreneurs had "invaded" the empire (or been invited in), developing railroads, textile mills, and Singer Sewing Machine dealerships.[4] Finally, when certain elements from the military, the palace, and the religious establishment cooperated in an abortive counterrevolution in April of 1909, Abdülhamid was deposed and Mehmed V Reşad was installed as sultan. Although Ottoman sultans would remain titular heads of the empire until the aftermath of World War I, never after Abdülhamid would they again wield sovereign power. That daunting responsibility passed to the cadre of military and civil bureaucrats who had brought about the 1908 revolution.

The new Ottoman regime, in the aftermath of the revolution, thus faced not only the difficult task of making constitutional government work, but also the task of surviving in the face of Western military and economic dominance. It was in these contexts of internal turmoil, external threat, and minimal censorship that Ottoman cartoonists framed their visions of the new and old Ottoman realities. Because of the complete absence of formal censorship in the period immediately after the revolution, one might characterize the summer and fall of 1908 as the period of most intense, most frivolous, most wild cartoon satire. After the 1908 revolution, satirists became the voices of Ottoman anxiety; and on this unstable ground they created a cartoon vision of the revolution.

Cartoons in the Revolutionary Era, 1908–1911

Cartoons of the revolutionary era can be characterized in a number of ways. First, there is no one, simple classification for these cartoons. They ranged, in style, from the primitive to the highly sophisticated.[5] Most were in shades of black and white, although a few of the more costly gazettes featured cartoons in color. Some relied on elaborate captions to get their messages across, others were direct and telling even without caption. Cartoonists were not confined to a single gazette; some worked in ateliers and others produced satiric frames for several gazettes at once.[6] And although some cartoonists were quite well known, many cartoons were anonymous, suggesting that the cartooning arts were neither so proprietary and exclusive nor so artist-centered as they are in the press of the latter twentieth century.

Ottoman cartoonists drew on various modes of satire for inspiration. Many were clearly influenced, in cartoon style, by the satiric presses of Europe (French, English, Italian, German).[7] But there is no evidence that "Europeans" were employed to ink Ottoman cartoons, which were, in the end, a uniquely Ottoman art form.[8] In part, that uniqueness derived from a compelling synthesis of "traditional" symbols and dialogic forms with a very "modern" set of circumstances and influences. For one thing, the dialog and characters of the traditional shadow puppet theater translated readily into the cartoon space; satiric dialog based on the repartee of the shadow puppet theater was ubiquitous in the cartoons of this era. In cartoons, one also finds the symbols of traditional kingship (the sultanic crown, the palace eunuchs, the sultan himself) juxtaposed to images of "modernity:" the airplane, the automobile, the parliamentary delegate. And, one finds images of traditional Ottoman society (the narghile, the baggy peasant pants, the veiled female, the coffeehouse) juxtaposed to images of the European cultural invasion: the big, feathered hat, the frock coat, the exposed bosom, the cafe-concert. Thus, Ottoman cartooning, while taking imitation in art for granted, created a distinctive, synthetic art form that was reflective of the political crises and radical social tranformations which characterized the Ottoman empire of that time.

Finally, the Ottoman cartoon space, as part of the still-developing print culture of the time, was not simply evocative of the ideas of the elite classes who formed the primary audience for the revolutionary gazettes. Cartoons transcended the boundaries of the literate and illiterate classes. They were passed around, hung on walls, and read aloud in the coffee shops.[9] Their language was often a language of the common and colloquial. The rituals and symbols of the illiterate classes were an inherent part of cartoon culture, and the language and characters (like Karagöz) of the shadow theater were shared across lines of class and literacy.

Old and New Woman in the Cartoon Space

The cartoons presented in this essay do not give a comprehensive picture of the images of woman in the Ottoman cartoon space. Those images were extremely varied whereas only a few examples can be presented here. Further, the selection of images for this essay was to a large degree determined by access to gazettes which could be photographed or digitally scanned.[10] Nonetheless, the images here do reflect a set of cartoon woman types which are found across a broad spectrum of Ottoman gazettes. They are figures which embody the dilemmas of societal change and which share common features with cartoon women in other places and other times. They are figures which symbolize the contrasts between the old and the new.

The press of this era saw Ottoman society as faced with, and compelled to articulate, a certain disjuncture between the old and the new that was both forced and welcome, both exciting and fearsome. There was considerable discussion in the press of the meanings and implications of the old (*eski*) and the new (*yeni*); within that frame, journalists mulled over the concepts of constitutionalism, freedom, sovereignty, and civilization. Numerous articles appeared with titles like: "Yesterday and Today," "The Former Era and the Present," "The Age of Despotism and the Age of Freedom."[11] References to these contrasts were ubiquitous in the pages of the serious and the satirical press as Ottomans pondered the evolution of a new Ottoman order of things. Such discussions had antecedents in similar debates in the empire dating back to the eighteenth century.

In cartoon frames, the contrast between old and new was also explored, and combined with juxtapositions of East and West, honor and shame, and glory and weakness, to produce a set of visions of the revolutionary situation. Neither the new nor the old was considered unilaterally good or unilaterally bad; each had its advantages. The cartoon space provided the images (faces, costumes, names, settings, mannerisms) to match these options for Ottoman identity.[12] It explored the questions of how the state would evolve, what it would look like, and how its society and citizens would behave. It imagined the extent to which the familiar old society would be altered by the new constitutional regime and by the increasingly pervasive influences of Europe. Satirists portrayed the empire as plagued by a social order which was neither old nor new, but both at once. Out of this context of comparison, they conjured a set of woman figures who embodied the old and the new. These figures were not fixed (although they relied on familiar and recognizable symbols to point up their identities); they evolved along with Ottoman society. They were a response to the revolutionary situation, its needs, its anxieties, its desire for self-definition.

There are, in any given culture, for a given time and situation, complex and multiple options for representing woman.[13] Ottoman cartoonists had at their disposal a multiplicity of woman images and cultural markers, some of long duration and others recently borrowed or assimilated. They utilized these images and markers both to reflect and to shape the Ottoman situation. This paper examines three of their *yeni* (new) woman figures and one *eski* (old). The first woman figure is what Şerif Mardin called the "super-Westernized" Ottoman and what Deniz Kandiyoti and others have called the *alafranga* woman. She is Europeanized, a figure alternately sinister, alluring, or ridiculous. She represents Ottoman womanhood sacrificed on the altar of European culture, or engaged as a willing partner in corrupting Ottoman society from within and sapping its strength and virility.[14] The other two new woman figures served, in part, as antidotes to the *alafranga* woman. One was "Türkiye," an allegorical figure of the nation, and the other was the sister-citizen, a patriot. Türkiye was the embodiment of Ottoman territorial and cultural integrity. The sister citizen was the opposite of the *alafranga* woman; she rejected or critically examined the lures and the threats of European culture, preserving at once her own honor (sexual, economic, and civic) and the honor of the nation. She was the bearer of the next generation of Ottoman citizen patriots.

The figure who represented the "past era" (*devr-i sabık*), and its "traditions" as against the onslaught of "modernity," constitutionalism, foreign influence, and *alafranga* culture, was the old nag, a timeless, frumpy, post-menopausal figure who took her stand in the public space and whose tongue was ready to take on the challenges and deficiencies of both old era and new. In many ways, she, as public spokeswoman and skeptic, was the female counterpart of Karagöz, the John Q. Public of the shadow puppet theatre, a figure who was ubiquitous in the Ottoman satirical press. As everywoman, a not-so-innocent bystander or folk-wise observer, the old nag suffered the agonies of cultural disruption, the exploitation of her labor, and the oppressive weight of government whether sultanic or constitutional.[15]

None of these woman figures was entirely new. Each had antecedents taken from the women of the Turkish shadow puppet theatre and from archetypical figures (like Marianne and Miss Liberty) of the Western revolutions which had influenced the Ottoman revolutionaries.[16] Their forms were mythic (the idealized symbols of freedom, the motherland, heroic tradition) and pedestrian (the woman at home or in the street). Türkiye and the sister-citizen had antecedents in literary figures like the female defenders of tribal honor, hearth, and family found in epics like the *Book of Dede Korkut*.[17] The *alafranga* woman was rooted in images of the foreign female, the temptress, and the sorceress found in such works as the Arabian Nights. The old nag was a standard trope of literatures worldwide: the wise old granny, the grumpy old mother, the voice of reason against the rashness of youth and invention.[18]

Each "new" woman figure also had an assumed and contrasting counterpart. The ideal figure of the heroic Türkiye was opposed to the earlier image of Türkiye brutalized by the tyranny of the sultanic regime. The sister-citizen was juxtaposed to a pre-revolutionary Ottoman female imagined to be less informed and less participant. The *alafranga* cartoon woman was opposed, on the one hand, to European womanhood, as separate and unequal sister, and, on the other hand, to a previous ideal of Ottoman womanhood (demure, unpolluted, dressed in traditional clothing, avoiding the public space). This is not to say that Europeanized women (those who adopted European fashions, language, education, manners, or entertainments) were universally criticized in Ottoman cartoons. In the satirical press, imitation of Western culture and consumption of Western goods could still be equated with progressive attitudes and material prosperity. Given, however, the precarious position of the empire at the time of the revolution, Europeanized women became an easy target and a readily identifiable symbol of the imbalance of power afflicting the Ottoman state in its relations with Europe.

The *Alafranga* Woman

The image of the new in Ottoman satire was often embodied in the figure of the *alafranga* (or Westernized) Ottoman. The *alafranga* woman figured prominently in a genre of Ottoman literature and imagery which criticized and made fun of those Ottomans (male and female) who adopted Western fashions, ideas, and manners wholesale.[19] These Westernized Ottomans were accused of slavish imitation, foolishness, conspicuous consumption, and endangering the sovereignty and cultural integrity of the empire.

The term *alafranga* was often coterminous with "modern" in the Ottoman satirical press. The "modern" young man and the "modern" young woman, modern socializing, modern marriage, and modern ideas in general were all fair game for the satirist's pen. They all symbolized the subordination of the Ottomans to European ways and the sometimes dizzying effects of the sociocultural transformation that Istanbul was experiencing.[20]

One gazette was even entitled *Alafranga*. It used as its mascots, on the masthead, the figures of a donkey couple [Figure 1].[21] Fashionably dressed, they sat opposite each other at a cafe table, wineglasses before them. They were consumers of European style and European entertainment.[22]

Figure 1

Satiric images of such cultural collaboration linked moral weakness to the consumption of European goods. European dress among upper class Ottomans had become commonplace by 1908 but, in the cartoon space, Paris fashion was an easy way to suggest luxury, frivolity, and a dearth of patriotic concern for the best interests of the empire. The journal *Alem* ran a poem (in French) which satirized the modern young Ottoman. He was, according to the poem, an insouciant and self-satisfied fop, who fancied himself a theatre critic, responded with indifference to the war in Bulgaria, and found it inconvenient to support the boycott against Austrian goods.[23] *Kalem* ran another poem, entitled "Décadent," in French, which satirized the paradox of the Occidentalized Ottoman who loved European theatre, styles, and food, but still drew the lines when it came to the cultural borders separating Ottoman and European.[24] Such *alafranga* dandies were the butts of many jokes. But it was one thing for Ottoman men to make themselves ridiculous following the European fashions and disporting themselves in cafes; it was quite another thing for Ottoman women to allow themselves similar liberties.

The *alafranga* Ottoman was associated with conspicuous consumption which, in turn, would sap the strength of the empire by sqandering its limited resources and by making it vulnerable to Europe. Consumption of European goods, in and of itself, was not universally condemned or caricatured in the press. But conspicuous consumption was satirized as a weakness to which Ottoman women were particularly prone; their consumption of European styles and the drain on financial resources which it entailed had to be restrained, as did their attraction to the *alafranga* lifestyle.[25] Ads in Ottoman gazettes touted imported hats, parasols, watches, and corsets; while Ottoman cartoons, sometimes in the same gazettes, lampooned the weakness of the *alafranga* female who consumed them.[26]

Just such a woman can be seen in a cartoon in *Kalem*. It shows a very fashionable *alafranga* couple chatting on the street [figure 2]. She wears a chic suit, a big hat, a stole, a parasol, and a muff. The man says, "What a chic outfit, my dear, how much did it cost you?" With a slight, sweet smile, she replies, " My husband gave me five lira, but it cost twenty."[27] The message in this frame is one of extravagance in the pursuit of European fashion. But it is more than that; the woman has circumvented the household budget and her husband's authority. She is also out in the

Figure 2

street; her relationship to the *alafranga* man is unclear, but he is decidedly not her husband.

Depicting the extravagance of women in elaborate or foreign fashions was not unique to the Ottoman cartoon space, it was also a commonplace of European satires. But in the Ottoman press, the dressing of women in European fashion, and hence the transforming of woman from merely frivolous to *alafranga* frivolous, meant something more. Women in extravagant dress could be characterized and dismissed as silly spendthrifts, but women in European dress symbolized cultural compromise, moral laxity, and economic subordination.

The *alafranga* style suggested a set of moral dilemmas which the "new" Ottoman society must face, like it or not.[28] The revolution, the empire's rapid social and political transformation, and the European cultural invasion were all perceived in Ottoman literature as contributing to a certain freedom which loosed women in new and disquieting ways. Deniz Kandiyoti, in her analysis of the Ottoman novel, has expressed the dilemma of Western influence in this way:

> . . . . in the Ottoman /Turkish novel the point of ultimate degradation is reached when Westernism, in the guise of foolish and feckless young men and 'fashionable' loose women, enters the home, corroding the moral fabric of the family and by extension the society as a whole.[29]

Although fashionable young men are represented, in the cartoon space as in the novel, as compromising the moral order of Ottoman society, it is the *alafranga* women who constitute the real threat to Ottoman morality; it is they who can corrupt absolutely. In literature, such women's behavior runs the gamut from "frivolous and inconsequential" to "truly corrupt," as illustrated in the turn of the century Ottoman novels *Felatun Beyle Rakım Efendi* and *Aşk-ı Memnu*.[30]

In the revolutionary cartoon, the *alafranga* woman was perhaps more often frivolous than truly corrupt. But because the integrity of Ottoman culture was always contingent upon the sexuality of its women and upon their providing a certain continuity in the ordering of society, the image of the frivolous, Westernized, exposed woman always had certain sinister connotations. She suggested a society at risk, a breaching of propriety,

Figure 3

and a violation of sexual boundaries.[31]

Cartoons of *alafranga* women were used to emphasize the perceived dichotomies between East and West. The Ottoman *alafranga* woman was intimately associated with her counterpart, the fashionable European woman, who was in turn associated with inappropriate dress and inappropriate behavior. Both types were a threat to the social and moral fabric. Ottoman men were depicted as dazzled by the allure of European fashion and by the women who wore it. In this type of representation, the threat to the Ottoman state and society was not an Ottoman woman in European fashion, but the seductive European woman herself. Imagining women of other cultures as seductive temptresses, of course, was nothing new. There had long been genres of literature which classified women according to their "nations" or traits; and Orientalist art made a business of imagining Middle Eastern temptresses, as is evident in the frontspiece of E. J. W. Gibb's 1901 *Ottoman Literature*, which depicts a "flower of the Orient," naked, legs akimbo, and lounging back in clear invitation.[32]

Ottoman cartoons of European women were a bit more restrained. But the message of availability was similar. Some cartoons depicted the Westernized "Young Turks" off in Paris or Vienna, wasting the energies (and money) of the nation on foreign women.[33] Sedad Nuri drew a cartoon showing a smiling Westernized "Young Turk" strolling with a fashionable young European, his arm encircling her shoulders and his hand beneath her breast [Figure 3]. He jokes, "And there are those who suppose I'm xenophobic" (*ecnebi düşmanı*).[34] The foreign women, in these frames, were fashionable and enticing, and the Ottoman men willingly susceptible. In other frames, cartoon seductresses, like the many European entrepreneurs who had flooded the empire seeking profit, supposedly worked their wiles in Istanbul, corrupting the young men of the Ottoman nation.[35] One cartoon showed two dapper young Ottomans dressed in the latest Paris fashion eyeing a fashionable young lady out for a stroll with her dog. "Don't ogle too long," warned one, "She's Austrian!"[36]

These images of foreign seductresses and their weak male admirers were complemented by the images of *alafranga* Ottoman women. The latter, who adopted European styles and the forms of entertainment that went with them, were implicated as guilty of the same types of loose behavior that were assumed to be commonplace among European

Figure 4

women.[37] If they would wear the kind of fashions that European women wore, then they would go out as European women did and mingle with men in ways that were not socially acceptable.

One cartoon, for example, shows two fashionable women conversing [Figure 4]. "A perfect cafe-concert is opening nearby in Pera [the European district of Istanbul]," says one. "What's that to me?" responds her companion. The first woman exclaims, "Really rich men will be going there," to which her companion replies, "What's that to you?"[38] In many ways this is a standard type of lampoon which targets women's catty and gold-digging behavior. But beyond that meaning is the suggestion that the *alafranga* woman would be circulating in the public space, pursuing men openly rather than utilizing more discreet or customary channels.

The link between sexuality and the *alafranga* woman is deftly illustrated in a cartoon in *Falaka* which depicts a direct comparison of the East with the West. This cartoon shows a large balance scale, one side labelled "East" (*Şark*), and one side labelled "West" (*Garb*). On the "Western" side are two fashionably dressed women and a crying child. On the "Eastern" side, there are also two women and a child holding a doll [Figure 5]. The "Eastern" women are dressed in a bastardized or semi-Western style, one wearing a filmy veil. The scale is tipped in favor of the "East." The caption reads: "The women of a nation should not simply be a measure of the degree of its progress; but a proof of the degree of its moral purity." The gazette's two male mascots stand next to the scale, smiling and pointing. The Falakacı excitedly congratulates his friend: "See that, Deli Oğlan! Ours again, ours are still heavier! [Life and] love to you!"[39]

This cartoon can be "read" at a number of levels. First of all, it clearly demonstrates the conscious and continuous weighing in the Ottoman press of the empire against Europe, and the critical role of women in that comparison. It also points up the marked yet incomplete Europeanization of women's styles, and shows the association of these styles with "progress." The crying child and her headless doll, on the Western side of the scale, suggest the problems that this "progress" may have brought the women of the West. The Ottoman women "outweighed" their European counterparts, but their "chastity" was still suspect. It had to be weighed. This cartoon points up the inclination in the satirical press to conflate

Figure 5

immorality and Westernized progress and to use *alafranga* dress as suggestive of moral decline. Beyond those representations, the cartoon proposes that progress (*terakki*) remained an area in which Ottoman women fell short of their European counterparts, and that, when it came to an issue of progress or chastity, Ottoman men preferred the women of the nation to be a measure of the latter. In an era marked by Ottoman subordination to Europe, Ottoman men could at least hope for cultural superiority through the purity of their women.

Woman as Nation

In the face of the *alafranga* woman, and the dominance of Europe which she represented, the Ottoman cartoon space needed a heroine, the female figure of the nation.[40] This female nation was named *Türkiye* (Turkey), *Hürriyet* (Freedom), or *Meşrutiyet* (Constitutionalism).[41] In the cartoon space, she embodied the ideals of freedom, integrity, vulnerability, community, and love. Ottoman cartoonists usually gendered other states, particularly those which posed threats to the empire, as males, often dressed in military uniform. Male nation figures tended to embody the qualities of aggression, militarism, power, imperialism, valor, lust, and greed. The Ottoman nation, on the other hand, while ordinarily portrayed as a mother or beloved, could also be embodied in the figures of the goverment, or of the noble Ottoman soldier, defender of the empire's territory and sovereignty.[42] Cartoon France, as model of revolution and symbol of freedom, was characterized as the voluptous Marianne. But when the France in question was a greedy European state, ambitious to exploit Ottoman resources or territory, it was invariably characterized as a short, unseemly male. The aggressive England was John Bull; and Austria, Russia, and Germany were personified by their rulers, by military figures with weapons, or by ferocious beasts. Perceived as threatening and rapacious, the states of Europe became virile, menacing, militaristic men in the Ottoman cartoon space. These male personifications of European states were the obvious counterpart to the female gendering of the Ottoman state. "She" was a mother, a wife, or a daughter, engendering patriotic sentiments through her need for protection and her guardianship of the national honor.[43] The juxtaposing of male and female nation figures is illustrated in a cartoon in *Malum*, where a female Türkiye confronts the "powers," the male figures of European states who are contending to own or entice her [Figure 6].[44] This image of the "balance" of power suggests the perceived risk inherent in Ottoman foreign affairs.

The female personification of the Ottoman nation was depicted as alternately beleaguered by her enemies, or defiant. Most often she appeared virginal or, if a wife and mother, at least a youthful one. Serenely she upheld the values and honor of the nation. Despotism and imperialism both constituted threats to her beauty, grace, and sexuality. In some frames, Türkiye warded off the European males; in others she was shown laid low, made ill, or even dismembered by internal and external threats.[45] She was often placed in juxtaposition to the male characters representing European nations, who were charged in the Ottoman press

Figure 6

with the cardinal sins of lust and gluttony. If these male aggressors were not shown attempting to seduce or carry off a female symbol of the nation, they were shown gobbling up the nation in one form or another.[46] Depictions of eating and of acts of physical or sexual aggression were readily identifiable and convenient ways to represent an imbalance of power between the Ottoman state and its enemies. When the nation was embodied in the female form, the vision of sexual dishonor was added to that of military dishonor.

These ultimately horrifying images, produced by men for a predominantly (but not exclusively) male audience, were designed to provoke feelings of humiliation, and to invoke a patriotic response.[47] When the brutal, sly, lustful, or greedy male figures of European nations looked upon her with desire, she demanded that the Ottomans come to her defense. Whether the danger came in the form of economic imperialism, European armies, cultural degradation, or tyranny at home, she was the motherland who offered the Ottomans the options of action or inaction, bravery or shame.[48]

Yet the mythical figure of woman as nation was not always defenseless, or dependent on a male protector.[49] She might be portrayed resisting, with dignity and grace, those who threatened her, or even flaunting her power joyously. Two cartoon examples serve to illustrate these alternatives. They also demonstrate how dress markers were used both to identify patriotic female archetypes, and to distinguish them from the alafranga woman types who compromised rather than upheld Ottoman honor.

The first cartoon juxtaposes "Liberty" (the new political order) to "Despotism" (the old sultanic regime).[50] Liberty is a serene and mature young female, dressed in classical draperies [Figure 7]. Her robes make her appear timeless, associated neither with an oppressive past nor an uncertain and Europeanized present. Despotism is an ugly monster, apparently tamed by Liberty. His body is bared and he has no markers of national type—he is a monster for all times. This cartoon shows the triumph of the female nation over the threat from within, the possibility that the old regime, associated with tyranny, will reassert itself against the new constitutional order. This frame is a commentary on what the Ottomans hope they have have achieved by their revolution.

The second cartoon is much more specific as to time and place, and

Figure 7

it represents the empire and the motherland as still engaged in struggle. The frame is dominated by a huge and smiling female Türkiye, dressed in traditional costume, breaking her chains, and dwarfing the tiny figures of her would-be European enslavers [Figure 8].[51] This woman's dress, and those of the men around her, mark each character as having a specific "national" identity. Her dress, a rather generic type of "peasant," ethno-national costume, marks her as clearly linked to a glorious Ottoman past, and as uncorrupted by "modern," *alafranga* fashion.[52] Her power, then, seems to lie in maintaining her traditional identities. This latter cartoon is one of the striking visual images produced by the idiosyncratic Mehmed Fazlı, editor of the journal *Lak Lak*, who drew most of his gazette's cartoons and is memorable for his biting social as well as political satire. Fazlı's female nation, in the form of *Meşrutiyet* (Constitutionalism), is shackled, but she is announcing to the world, and to the male caricatures of European states gazing up at her, that she will no longer bear the burden of her chains which are labelled *cehalet* (ignorance/folly/naivete/childishness) and *imtiyazat* (the capitulations). These burdens are highly significant.[53] Ignorance, folly, and childishness were associated with women (in classical and contemporary literatures), but this mythic female figure of the Ottoman state could now transcend those disabilities. It was often only in such mythic form that the satirical press could envision Ottoman womankind actually freed from the ignorance which held her in a child-like state.[54] But, in images like this one, the female figure, without male protectors, is used to voice the defiance and "independence" of the Ottoman nation, newly reborn as a constitutional regime, and impatient with European dominance. The capitulations, one-sided economic treaties imposed on the empire by the various states of Europe, especially England and France, symbolized the empire's economic dependence. Without breaking the "chains" of the capitulations, the empire would remain doomed inevitably to economic subordination. Thus, the female nation here represents both hope and resistance. She is a "new" woman in an "old" costume, which stands for the past economic power and autonomy of the Ottomans. She could not throw off the Austrian, English, and French enslavers if she were wearing the European costume which symbolized her commercial and cultural dependence.

Figure 8

The Sister-Citizen

The female nation on a more human scale was embodied in the person of the sister-citizen. She was the antithesis of the *alafranga* woman, a patriot who would stand by the empire as best she could, although not always in the same way as her male counterpart. The sister-citizen is not so much a feature of the Ottoman cartoon space as the other three women types mentioned, perhaps because she was neither so glorious as the allegorical Türkiye, nor so potentially destructive as the *alafranga* woman. In the rhetoric of revolutionary gazettes, however, she is found often enough, addressed along with her "brother" citizens in narratives prompting the Ottomans to patriotic action.[55]

The sister-citizen can be found in cartoon frames, often in the form of the "every-day" woman who is doing what she can for the nation and avoiding the types of extravagant dress and behavior that the *alafranga* woman indulged in. Sister-citizens are wives, mothers, and workers; they are found in the cartoon space in the form of women who participate in the boycott against Austrian goods.[56] One sister-citizen is found among her male counterparts, "contributing" her scanty resources to a government-sponsored fund in a cartoon in *Lak Lak* which critiques the negligent and tight-fisted behavior of the rich in comparison to the constant "giving" of the poor.[57] Cartoon women could be constructive citizens in a variety of ways; they chipped in, they suffered government levies without grumbling, they were good and loyal wives, they did not consume extravagantly. The sister-citizen represented consent and cooperation in the modernizing, liberating project of the nation.[58] She was a wife and mother, she was frugal and sensible, she read the papers or listened to her husband's advice on the progress of the nation.[59] She valued education and would raise nation-loving children.

The juxtaposition of such females to males in the cartoon space tended to place them under the guidance of their men.[60] But some cartoon frames were women-only situations. Woman power, for the citizen-patriot, often came in the forms of economic or social self-restraint, but it also came in the form of childbearing, the production of new citizen-patriots.[61] A characteristic Ottoman cartoon which focuses on the notion of motherhood as defining the citizen-patriot also illustrates the use of dress markers to signify the division between those women who support the empire and those who threaten it. This cartoon, entitled *nesli cedid* (New Generation), shows a young mother with her baby in a cradle at her side [Figure 9]. The child is dressed in a fez and holding a rifle. Two jovial young women address her, "Sister, may you be spared. Is it a girl or a boy?" The mother answers, "A soldier, by God!"[62] Through her reproduc-

Figure 9

tion and nurturing roles, this Ottoman cartoon mother at once serves her own patriotic duty and creates a new generation of soldier citizen-patriots.[63] To emphasize the point of their patriotic Ottoman-ness, all three women are dressed in exaggeratedly "traditional" costume. Like the gigantic *Meşrutiyet* of the *Lak Lak* cartoon, illustrated earlier, there is no mistaking their identity. They are *Ottoman* sister-citizen mothers.[64] There is nothing *alafranga* about them. Their costumes suggest the glories of the past; but they are new women. The child, the new generation, will translate those glories into a military power of the future—a baby soldier to protect the motherland.[65]

The Old Nag

In addition to the mother-nation and the mother-citizen, Ottoman satire also proferred a different kind of mother to articulate the cartoon space's images of nation and revolution. This mother was not new; indeed she was imagined to be as old, as timeless, as time itself, and as the struggles of states and the trials of womankind. She represented the *eski* (old) side of the equation in the satirical press' images of woman. She was the old nag, who spoke a transcendant and universal wisdom. She was not the mythic madonna mother of the nation, holding the infant "Freedom" in her arms, but the scarred and skeptical mother whose children had grown up, and not turned out right. She was the long-suffering, enduring Jane Q. Public, viewing the revolution with jaundiced eye, who had yet to solve the dilemmas of the old hegemonies, much less to address the bewildering array of new cultural options and their effects. This cartoon mother was not fooled by the euphoria or the promises of "Liberté, Egalité, Fraternité." She knew that Europe's assault on the empire was only the latest in an endless cycle of the strong imposing their will upon the weak. She was the mirror image of the male everyman, Karagöz (the shadow puppet hero). She thought European influences could be good, bad, or indifferent—but the human condition remained the same. For her, virtue was a problematic construct and nation was a false construct. Feminism, like nationalism, might be a bum deal. This mother was satire's answer to the idealized vision of revolution. She asked the reader to remember suf-

Figure 10a

fering, want, and folly. She was the voice and image of the fears of the revolution, of the cultural anxiety which considered the threats faced by the empire: the undermining of its bases for social unity, its political ineptitude, and its economic dependence. Like her shadow puppet predecessors for generations past, she expected the worst.

The old nag came in different forms. Her figures were utilized in satiric dialog, humorous skits, and cartoons. But always she had an insistent voice.[66] In satiric dialog, she might be *Büyük Hanım* (Old Lady or Granny), bemoaning conditions for the woman (and man) in the street: bridge tolls, the price of bread, the fact that the government's loudly touted *hürriyet* (freedom) did not seem to bring the promised benefits.[67] The old nag's image appeared in the mastheads of several gazettes [Figure 10]. For example, the masthead of the periodical *Geveze* (Blabbermouth) contains two characters: one a jovial and talkative man, the other a scowling and scolding old woman [Figure 10a].[68] A similar image is found in the "Weekly Smile" section of the gazette, *Hande*, a dialog illustrated by an old man and an old woman gossiping over a fence.[69] The figure of the old nag gave the public in the Ottoman cartoon space a female as well as a male voice .

Foremost among the gazettes employing the old nag figure as a mascot was the gazette titled *Cadaloz*.[70] The gazette's mascot, Cadaloz [Figure 10b], had one of the most scathing tongues in the satirical press; she was middle-aged to elderly and aggressive.[71] The figure of Cadaloz suggests that with age comes a certain license. Indeed, the daring voice in Ottoman satire is often an aging voice. With age, too, comes a certain blurring of the lines between women (who may then be viewed as something besides sexual beings) and men.[72] Cadaloz was a strikingly androgynous figure. Freed from a sexual role, she was perhaps also free to take on what was ordinarily a male voice, a venomous satiric voice, in what

Figure 10b

was ordinarily a male space. Perhaps it is the assimilation of old women to men that allows her to be so outspoken. Perhaps it is her post-menopausal condition (freeing her from the constraints operative with sexually active and reproductive women) that gives her a dominant satiric voice, neither submissive victim nor extravagant consumer. Or perhaps her age is equated with wisdom.[73] Her dress (a significant indicator of character in cartoons) also approximated male dress in certain ways, in direct contrast to that of many Ottoman cartoon women which often exaggerated sexuality and femininity.

Cadaloz becomes the symbol *par excellence* of the skeptical voice which Ottoman cartoon satire applied to revolution, constitutionalism, and social transformation. She represents the disgust and discouragement of the public, and has no faith in the benevolence of political and social transformation. The old nag figure does not provoke directly the sense of shame and compromised male sexual honor which the beautiful or sexual female figures of the nation, like Türkiye, are designed to inspire. While her words may be shaming and castigating, they are spoken with irony. Unlike Türkiye, Cadaloz anticipates that the male nation will respond to shame with a hung head and a plea for patience. She expects inertia rather than action.

One cartoon in *Cadaloz* showed the old nag in her role as skeptical and street-wise observer of the ideals of revolution. In the frame there are three figures: *bir chic* (an *alafranga* dandy) in striped trousers, bow tie, and goosehead umbrella; a young street sweeper, virile and aggressive, in "traditional" dress; and, the sole female, the old nag. The street sweeper sweeps dirt on Mr. Chic's clothes. "Hey, you've soiled me, is this your idea of cleaning?" yells the dandy. "What are you yelling about?" retorts the young man, "There is *hürriyet* (freedom) for everyone now. I'll sweep any way I want!" In the background, the old nag shrugs: "Ah . . . we'll never get used to this freedom business . . . . we just don't understand it."[74] Here Cadaloz represents the "old" in dress and ideology. She identifies with neither of the male incarnations of the "new" empire: the nationalist street sweeper or the Europeanized *efendi*. She has neither sympathy for the overlay of European progress on the backs of the old military bureacratic class, nor for the young man's idealized vision of revolution.

Another example of the old nag in the Ottoman cartoon space juxta-

Figure 11

poses the old nag as mother to the *alafranga* woman as daughter [Figure 11]. The *alafranga* daughter, dressed fashionably in European style, complete with big hat, is headed out the door. Her grimacing and lumpish mother, in dress and apron, demands to know where she is going. "Skating, Mama," she replies, "The chicest men of Beyoğlu [a European district] gather there every evening."[75]

This cartoon targets a real social phenomenon in Istanbul at the time. Skating (both ice and roller) was becoming popular.[76] The gazette *Kalem* advertised a "Skating Palace" in Beyoğlu, which was "open every day to families in the morning and at noon times and, in the evenings, to the public."[77]

The skating palace was a good metaphor for Ottoman society's paradoxes of old and new.[78] The juxtaposition of the old and new in this cartoon pits the old nag, as defender of morality and traditional values, against the *alafranga* woman as symbol of a new generation that is modern, fashionable, looking for entertainment, relatively "free," and following its European counterpart down the path of immorality. The skating palace provided an opportunity for the young to pierce the boundaries of controlled sexual mingling, to see and be seen by strangers. It was Western, it was modern, it was "fast."

The *alafranga* daughter was a symbol of the ways in which European fashions (in dress and entertainment) compromised the integrity of Ottoman society. Proper young women did not go out in public alone seeking strange men, chic or otherwise. Public mingling of the sexes, in 1908 Istanbul, was viewed by some as signifying freedom, modernity, and progress, but by many others it was viewed as signifying license, immorality, and a chaotic disruption of the boundaries of patriarchal and familial authority.[79] Istanbul society was engaged in a dramatic period of social transformation. But Ottoman society was a long way from being comfortable with women frequenting skating palaces alone.

That discomfort was clearly in evidence in 1910 when an entrepreneur obtained a permit for a combined cinema and roller skating rink in Izmir.[80] Two afternoons a week were reserved for women. This drew considerable criticism, particularly in the press.

Articles appeared every day, one after another, to the effect that the sanctity of the home was being endangered, and that women would lose all sense of decency if allowed to view immodest pictures or, worse still, disport themselves on wheels.[81]

Apparently, fragile female sensibilities, at least to some observers, were not up to the moral challenge of skating; nor was the Ottoman household willing to become "modern" if modern meant the *alafranga* phenomena of rinks and cinemas for the ladies.

No wonder that the old nags of the satirical press were represented as long-suffering and skeptical of the advantages of European style "progress." Ten years after the Young Turk Revolution, the empire would surrender to the victorious European powers. In the aftermath of World War I, a new Ottoman gazette, *Diken*, would also feature an old nag as its mascot.[82] She cast a jaundiced eye on the suggestive antics of a new generation of *alafranga* Ottoman women. The fears of her predecessor, Cadaloz, had been all too real. Not only was the empire subordinated militarily by the armies of Europe, but it had been even further afflicted with European-style culture; it was overrun by *alafranga* daughters.

The Ottoman press' characterization of the old nag suggests that the struggle against imperialism and the dichotomy between *alafranga* woman, on the one hand, and mythic heroines or sister-citizens, on the other, do not suffice to comprehend the Ottoman satiric vision of woman and revolution.[83] Cadaloz is perhaps the most powerful image, the most compelling voice, among the woman forms in the Ottoman satirical press. She does not defend Islam, the monarchy, or the republic. She knows that the revolution will not bring glory or readily disarticulate customary social bounds. She is neither enamored of the constitutional project nor deceived by the illusion of her own role in it. She has been engaged in the patriarchal bargain for many generations.[84] And when she imagines woman, community, and nation, she believes that she knows them already, and that there is no such thing as progress, only change.

Notes

1. I am grateful to Mr. Joe Rader and Ms. Hua Li of the University of Tennessee Archive for the production of the digitally scanned cartoons used

in this article. This study is part of a work in progress entitled *Image and Imperialism in the Ottoman Revolutionary Press*, which focuses on gazettes published in Istanbul between 1908 and 1911.

2. Abdülhamid was not actually deposed until the following year, but after July 1908 he no longer actually controlled the government. The revolution was not a mass revolt and it did not radically alter Ottoman society immediately, but it did establish constitutional government, radically reduce the power of the sultan, and provide opportunities for a wide range of social transformations.

3. On which see: Feroz Ahmad, *The Young Turks: The Committee of Union and Progress in Turkish Politics 1908–1914* (Oxford: Clarendon Press, 1969); and Erik Zürcher, *The Unionist Factor: The Role of the Committee of Union and Progress in the Turkish National Movement, 1905–1926* (Leiden: E.J. Brill, 1984).

4. On Singer, see Robert Bruce Davies, *Peacefully Working to Conquer the World: Singer Sewing Machines in Foreign Markets, 1854–1920* (New York: Arno Press, 1976), pp. 206–220.

5. The study of the Ottoman press and of Ottoman satire is still in its primitive stages. The most comprehensive work available on Ottoman cartooning, a reference work, is Turgut Çeviker, *Gelişim Sürecinde Türk Karikatürü*, 3 vols. (İstanbul: Adam Yayınları, 1986–1991). For a more interpretive work on Arab cartooning of a later vintage, see Allen Douglas and Fedwa Malti-Douglas, *Arab Comic Strips: Politics of an Emerging Mass Culture* (Bloomington: Indiana University Press, 1994). For a pioneering study on the Arab press, which might serve as a model for work on the Ottoman press, see Ami Ayalon, *The Press in the Arab Middle East: A History* (New York: Oxford University Press, 1995).

6. There were at least two cartoon ateliers, "Soresco" and "İttihad ve Terraki Atelyesi," operating in Istanbul at this time. Turgut Çeviker, *Gelişim Sürecinde*, v. 2: 101–131, lists thirty-eight identifiable cartoonists (including one woman) active in the period 1908–1918 for whom some biographical information is available, and thirty-nine others who are partly identifiable but about whom we have little or no data at all.

7. Some gazettes, like *Kalem*, regularly reprinted European cartoons. See, for example, *Kalem*, 66: 3, 3 Kanun-ı evvel 1325/16 December 1909, which shows a cartoon taken from a Berlin gazette. The caption above this cartoon section says: *"Ecnebi karikatürlerinden"* (from the foreign cartoons).

8. The fact that some Ottoman cartoonists have apparently "European" names, like Scarselli or Rigopulos, should not be confused with the notion that Ottoman cartoons were produced by Europeans. The empire was a poly-eth-

nic and polyglot entity of long standing. Ottomans had many sorts of names and the cartoonists were overwhelmingly Ottoman citizens, although some may have been foreign nationals resident in Istanbul.

9. For an interesting analysis of modes of circulation and the use of coffee shops as venues for the sharing of gazettes with the non-literate, see Ayalon, *The Press in the Arab Middle East*, pp. 145–159. See also Beth Baron, "The Construction of National Honor in Egypt," *Gender and History* v. 5, no. 2: 244–255. Baron emphasizes the significance of oral expression in the dissemination of the idea of nationalism to a mostly illiterate populace. But I think she isolates print culture too rigidly as elite culture when, in fact, print culture, especially in the form of cartoons, was widely shared across boundaries of class and literacy.

10. The majority of the cartoons are from *Kalem*, a relatively sophisticated gazette aimed at an Ottoman audience bilingual in Ottoman and French. *Kalem* utilized a wide range of cartoonists, cartooning styles and cartoon targets.

11. For some varied examples, see Celal Nuri, *Türk İnkılabı* (İstanbul: Ahmed Kamil Matbaası, n.d.), pp. 130–140; *Volkan* 28: 1, 15 Kanun-ı sani 1324/28 January 1909; *Resimli Kitab* 1: 53–60, Eylül 1324/September 1908; and *İttifak* 11: 1–4, 14 Ağustos 1324/27 August 1908.

12. While discussing the drawing of identities here, it is important to note that the satirical press tended not to focus on the brotherhood of Muslims (while it did often focus on the brotherhood of the oppressed or the brotherhood of those suffering from imperialism). There were gazettes with a pointedly Islamic message, such as *Volkan*, but they were not satirical. In fact, although there were some cartoons satirizing various denominations, in general the satirical press avoided Islam as a direct theme or a direct target. One might argue that journalists avoided satirizing Islam out of piety, but perhaps a better explanation is that Islam provided one of the few remaining bases for social unity and the satirical press was preoccupied with targets which undermined Ottoman unity. Islam might be indirectly satirized by targeting the uneducated bumpkin type who was always calling upon Allah or by targeting religious superstitions. It is also important to note that Islam did not stand in the way of the production or consumption of cartoon images by a predominantly Muslim population. By 1908, cartooning in the empire was fairly sophisticated and its portrayal of subjects, like semi-nude women and sexual inuendo, much freer than, for example, press cartooning in Iran at the same time.

13. Partha Chatterjee, "The Nationalist Resolution of the Women's Question," in Kumkum Sangari and Sudesh Vaid, eds., *Recasting Women: Essays in*

Indian Colonial History (New Brunswick: Rutgers University Press, 1990), pp. 233–253, is a very interesting article on the case of the woman question and Indian nationalism, which tackles this question of standard dichotomies vs. the fluid nature of nationalist situations and the multiple images available for characterizing woman's place: "In fact, from the middle of the nineteenth century right up to the present day, there have been many controversies about the precise application of the home/world, spiritual/material, feminine/masculine dichotomies in various matters concerning the everyday life of the 'modern' woman . . . . the specific solutions were drawn from a variety of sources—a reconstructed 'classical' tradition, modernized folk forms, the utilitarian logic of bureaucratic and industrial practices, the legal idea of equality in a liberal democratic state. The content of the resolution was neither predetermined nor unchanging, but its form had to be consistent with the system of dichotomies which shaped and contained the nationalist project." (pp. 243–244).

14. Şerif Mardin, "Super Westernization in Urban Life in the Ottoman Empire in the Last Quarter of the Nineteenth Century," pp. 403–446 in Peter Benedict et. al., eds., *Turkey: Geographic and Social Perspectives*, Social, Economic and Political Studies of the Middle East Series, no. IX (Leiden: E. J. Brill, 1974); Deniz Kandiyoti, "Slave Girls, Temptresses, and Comrades: Images of Women in the Turkish Novel," *Feminist Issues* 8 (Spring 1988): 35–50.

15. There are other manifestations, many nameless, of the Jane Q. Public figure. But the old nag, named or nameless, is the most prevalent character of this type.

16. On Miss Liberty figures, see Linda Kerber, *Women of the Republic: Intellect and Ideology in Revolutionary America* (New York: W.W. Norton and Company, 1986), pp. 34–40, 71–72, 265–286, passim. On the iconography of Marianne, see Maurice Agulhon, *Marianne into Battle: Republican Imagery and Symbolism in France, 1789–1880* (Cambridge: Cambridge University Press, 1981).

17. Images of women in classical Middle Eastern literatures are complex; they varied as did the images of woman figures in the Ottoman satirical press. Along with the silly and conniving women associated with the Arabian Nights tales, we also have the noble and sacrificing figure of Sheherazade or the ferocious yet sensitive figure of Burla Hatun in the epic of *Dede Korkut*, who must agree (if unhappily) to eat the fried flesh of her own son rather than reveal her identity and sacrifice her virtue to marauding "infidels." Burla Hatun is a classical noble mother figure who symbolizes the defense not only of her personal honor, but that of her menfolk, tribe, and religion. See Faruk Sümer, Warren Walker, and Ahmet Uysal, eds., *The Book of Dede*

Korkut: A Turkish Epic (Austin: University of Texas Press, 1991), pp. 30–34.

18. Even in the face of formidable foreign threats, the options for representing Ottoman women were not limited to the poles of goddess or victim. R. Radhakrishnan, "Nationalism, Gender, and the Narrative of Identity, " in Andrew Parker et. al., eds., *Nationalisms and Sexualities* (New York: Routledge, 1992), p. 85, has suggested that: "Unable to procure its own history in response to its inner sense of identity, nationalist ideology sets up Woman as victim and goddess simultaneously." This is certainly the case in the Ottoman cartoon space; but the victims and goddesses serve alternate rhetorical purposes, and they are only two of the possible options for gendering the Ottoman nation. The old nag image, for example, does not conform to this dichotomy; she is a characteristic element of the Ottoman identity and Ottoman history and, as such, there is a certain security and comfort to her character between the poles of the "goddess" Türkiye and the "victim" (either duped collaborator or powerless Türkiye). See Sucheta Mazumdar, "Moving Away from a Secular Vision? Women, Nation and the Cultural Construction of Hindu India," in Valentine Moghadam, *Identity, Politics and Women: Cultural Reassertions and Feminisms in International Perspective* (Boulder: Westview Press, 1994), pp. 243–273, for another example of the construction of Indian woman as " . . . the repository of this national spiritual essence; a 'goddess' who must remain untainted by 'modernization' and its implied pollution" (p. 257).

19. The pioneering article on women and fashion in Ottoman cartoons of the nineteenth century was written by Nora Şeni, "19. Yüzyıl Sonunda İstanbul Mizah Basınında Moda ve Kadın Kıyafetleri," pp. 43–67 in Şirin Tekeli, *Kadın Bakış Açısından 1980'ler Türkiye'sinde Kadın* (İstanbul: İletişim Yayınları, 1990).

20. "Modern" was usually glossed *yeni* but also sometimes *moderne*. On "modern" notions of marriage see *Alem* 12: 14 (French section) reporting on a purported marriage in Chicago at the top of the Auditorium tower (the couple had to take the elevator to get there). For later satire on "modern" marriage, see the gazette *Diken*, published 1918–1920.

21. *Ala Franga* 1:1, 30 Teşrin-i sani 1326/12 December 1910. This gazette was one of several that were often criticized as scandalous but very popular (including the gazette entitled *Eşek*, published 1910–1912), which used the donkey (*eşek*) mascot in various forms.

22. This theme of satirizing the *alafranga* Ottoman dated to the nineteenth century and was, in fact, a popular topic in late-nineteenth-century Ottoman theater productions. See Metin And, *A History of Theatre and Popular*

Entertainment in Turkey (Ankara: Forum Yayınları, 1963–1964), p. 80. Carter Findley, *Bureacratic Reform in the Ottoman Empire: The Sublime Porte, 1789–1922* (Princeton: Princeton University Press, 1980), pp. 165–167, 208–211, comments on the different sorts of *alafranga* Ottoman official and on the differing degrees to which Westernization affected the political ideology and the public image of Ottoman officials. He distinguishes between true "modernists" and those "for whom modernity meant little more than glibness in French and the aping of Parisian manners and fashions" (p. 210). Carter Findley, *Ottoman Civil Officialdom: A Social History* (Princeton: Princeton University Press, 1989), pp. 174–210, contains a fairly elaborate discussion of the cultural dualism and intellectual orientations of the Ottoman official class.

23. *Alem* 2: 15 (French section), 5 Şubat 1324/18 February 1909.

24. *Kalem* 2: 11, 28 Ağustos 1324/10 September 1908.

25. No systematic study has been done on the subject of Ottoman consumption and the marketing of goods at this time. A survey of advertising in the Istanbul press might be a good place to start although a study of wills might also prove useful. For an interesting study (using notarial records) on the consumption and marketing of goods in Paris and on the consumption of elite-type goods by the lower classes, see Cissie Fairchilds, "The Production and Marketing of Populuxe Goods in Eighteenth-Century Paris, " pp. 228–248, in Brewer and Porter, *Consumption and the World of Goods.* Fairchilds traces (e.g. pp. 230, 235–239) the consumption of such goods as watches, pets, umbrellas, canes, and stockings. All of these goods were used to identify European style fashion in the Ottoman cartoon space.

26. Ottoman gazettes are full of ads for European and American products which are equated with the fashionable, the progressive, and the modern. American-made timepieces, for example, were advertised, "for 80 kuruş, from the most famous American factories," in *Serbesti. Serbesti* 144: 4, 28 Mart 1325/10 April 1909. *Kalem* advertised European clothing and corsets: *Kalem* 114: 14–15, 10 Şubat 1326/23 February 1911. These ads were aimed at the relatively well-to-do consumer.

27. *Kalem* 115: 6, 17 Şubat 1326/2 March 1911. The French caption of Figure 2 gives the total amount the outfit cost as "ten" liras whereas the Ottoman caption says "twenty" liras. See also *Kalem* 114: 10, 10 Şubat 1326/23 February 1911, for a cartoon lampooning an *alafranga* woman who shows up at a ball shortly after her husband dies rather than staying home in mourning.

28. Woman as symbolizing the moral fabric of society and of the family is, of course, a theme which crosses cultural, national, class, and racial bound-

aries. Much work has been done on the social construction of female identity and the imposition of morality in colonial context, but Ottoman historiography, in general, has left those territories relatively unexplored. Some steps have been taken in this direction by Duben and Behar, *Istanbul Households*, see especially Ch. 7, pp. 194–238, on "Westernization and New Family Directions: Cultural Reconstruction." For examples of work on other areas of the world see, for example: Andrew Parker et. al., eds., *Nationalisms and Sexualities* (New York: Routledge, 1992); Kumkum Sangari and Sudesh Vaid, eds., *Recasting Women: Essays in Indian Colonial History* (New Brunswick: Rutgers University Press, 1990); Valentine Moghadam, ed., *Identity, Politics, and Women: Cultural Reassertions and Feminisms in International Perspective* (Boulder: Westview Press, 1994); and Haleh Afshar, ed., *Women, State and Ideology: Studies from Africa and Asia* (London: Macmillan, 1987).

29. Deniz Kandiyoti, "Slave Girls, Temptresses, and Comrades: Images of Women in the Turkish Novel," *Feminist Issues* 8 (Spring 1988): 38.

30. Kandiyoti, op. cit., pp. 38, 41–42, uses this concept of the *alafranga* woman to good effect in her treatment of literary "heroines." *Felatun Beyle Rakım Efendi* was published in 1875 by Ahmed Mithat and *Aşk-ı Memnu* in 1900 by Halit Ziya Uşaklıgil. Domestic dramas, such as those treated by Kandiyoti, and stories were popular in the periodical press of the revolutionary period. They could be either serious or satirical.

31. Aileen Ribeiro, *Dress and Morality* (New York: Holmes & Meier Publishers, 1986), has created a brief illustrated historical survey of some of the ways in which dress, sex, sin, and morality have been treated in Western art. She quotes the 1931 publication, "Modest Apparel," that says, "Suggestive dress means in the end the ruin of a people" (p. 146). That notion might be modified in the context of 1908 Istanbul to include the suggestion that Western dress (often synonymous with suggestive dress) might prove to be the ruin of a people. Ribeiro also cites the 1906 work of a Jesuit, Father Bernard Vaughan, entitled *The Sins of Society*, which "castigated those in the 'Smart Set,' whose craving for sports, pleasures, travel and immodest dress indicated a reversal to paganism" (p. 146). These arguments clearly demonstrate that the concerns over morality, entertainment, and dress expressed in the Ottoman revolutionary press were not limited to Ottoman, Asian, or Muslim contexts.

32. Elias J. W. Gibb, *Ottoman Literature* (New York: M. Walter Dunne, 1901), frontispiece. For a different take on cartoon females as oversexed "other," this time an American version of the Latin temptress, see Julianne Burton, "Don (Juanito) Duck and Imperial-Patriarchal Unconscious: Disney Studios, the Good Neighbor Policy, and the Packaging of Latin America," pp. 21–41,

in Andrew Parker et. al., eds., *Nationalisms and Sexualities* (New York: Routledge, 1992).

33. This work deals only with one set of images signifying the subordination of the empire to European interests. Perhaps an even more prevalent set of images was that showing the symbolic exploitee as a chicly dressed member of the government.

34. *Kalem* 100: 10, 21 Teşrin-i evvel 1326/4 December 1910. "Xenophobic" has other connotations than what is said here, literally "enemy of foreigners" or "anti-foreign," but it does express the notion of hostility to people and things non-Ottoman. This cartoon looks as though a bit of ink may have been added to obscure the exact position of the "gentleman's" hand beneath the "lady's" breast. Findley, *Ottoman Civil Officialdom*, p. 224, points out that Abdülhamid had forbidden Muslim dependents to accompany Ottoman ambassadors abroad and this surely encouraged liasons with foreign women. Or, as Findley rather delicately puts it: "This prohibition may have increased the frequency of marriages—and less formal liasons—between Ottoman diplomats and foreign ladies, some of them unsuitable choices, with the result that a decree issued after the 1908 revolution required all Foreign Ministry officials to obtain approval from the ministry for their marriages."

35. Such themes were also reflected in the novels of the late Ottoman period, as suggested by Deniz Kandiyoti, "Slave Girls, Temptresses," p. 42. Kandiyoti mentions the novel *Mürebbiye* (The Governess), by Hüseyin Rahmi Gürpınar, published in 1898, "where the importation of Mlle Angèle, a French governess, for the sake of fashion, into a traditional Ottoman household results in a farcical denoument where family honor and propriety are totally compromised." A Moroccan diplomat in mid-nineteenth-century Paris, remarking on the fashions and (corset-induced) figures of the Parisian women, suggested that the fashionable European woman was almost irresistable: "If one of them is close to you, you are seized with the desire to grab her by the waist." See Muhammad Saffar, *Disorienting Encounters: Travels of a Moroccan Scholar in France in 1845–1856*, trans. by Susan Miller (Berkeley: University of California Press, 1992), pp. 182–183.

36. *Kalem* 8: 10, 9 Teşrin-i evvel 1324/22 October 1908. Many cartoons also showed Ottomans abroad consorting with foreign women.

37. On representations of European women in Iranian literatures at this time, and their use in constructing Iranian women images, see Mohamad Tavakoli-Targhi, "Women of the West Imagined: The *Farangi* Other and the Emergence of the Woman Question in Iran," in Moghadam, *Identity, Politics and Women*, pp. 98–122.

38. *Kalem* 102: 3, 4 Teşrin-i sani 1326/17 November 1910.

39. *Falaka* 3: 4, 1 Ağustos 1327/14 August 1911. *İffet* can be translated as chastity, uprightness, or purity.

40. The Ottoman nation was ordinarily gendered as female in the cartoon space.

41. See, for example, *Falaka* 8: 1 [date is approximately 18 Ağustos 1327/31 August 1911], for an idealized representation of *hürriyet* as a beautiful female fairy. The term *Türkiye*, was fairly commonly and traditionally used for the Ottoman empire even though it extended (still in 1908) considerably beyond the boundaries of the Anatolian peninsula; this designation does not imply the modern nation-state of Turkey and its post World War I boundaries. See Linda Kerber, *Women of the Republic*, esp. pp. 80–110, for the feminization of the nation in the case of the United States. Images of states and territory embodied as women continued in the Ottoman satirical press after the fall of the empire, as strikingly illustrated on the cover of *Papağan* 38: 1, 7 Kanun-ı sani 1341/January 20, 1925, where the female is the object of a lustful "Red" Russia.

42. For example, see *Nekregu ile Pişekar* 3: 1, 3 Haziran 1325" 16 June 1909, for the Ottoman state as soldier rescuing a half-naked female figure who represents Crete.

43. Parts of the empire could also take on this female personification: for example, Crete in one cartoon is shown as a pretty young woman, in exaggerated "native" dress, being led off by lustful European male soldiers, *Kalem* 52: 8, 27 Ağustos 1325/9 September 1909. Crete's status was still contested at this time and Ottoman cartoons tended to represent "her" as still the empire's property, although that was not, in fact, the case.

44. *Malum* 2: 1, 10 Kanun-ı evvel 1326/23 December 1910.

45. The empire was often shown as a sick patient (male or female) being cut up or done in by evil or ignorant physicians. For one example of the sick mother Türkiye, see *Kalem* 76: 5, 18 Şubat 1325/March 2 1910.

46. See *Kalem* 10: 7, 23 Teşrin-i evvel 1324" 5 November 1908, for Austria, as a dirty old man, trying to lure off two young girls in peasant costume, probably meant to represent the Ottoman Balkan provinces of Bosnia and Herzegovina. Ottoman cartoons also used the examples of other areas (Iran, Egypt, Morocco, or India) which were subject to the appetites of various European imperialists: *Kalem* 99: 14, 14 Teşrin-i evvel 1326/27 October 1910.

47. Patriotic imagery in the context of war is the subject of Müge Göçek, "From Empire to Nation: Images of Women and War in Ottoman Political Cartoons, 1908–1923," in Billie Melman, ed., *Borderlines: Gender and Identities in Peace and War (1880–1030)* (London: Routledge, forthcoming). Göçek speculates on the reasons why some of women's activities were

exaggerated and others were ignored in the context of wartime representation.

48. Such representations of a vulnerable and threatened female nation were not unique to the Ottoman cartoon space; they are a longstanding commonplace of the visual and poetic imageries designed to mobilize a populace for defense or for aggression. See, for example: Samita Sen, "Motherhood and Mothercraft: Gender and Nationalism in Bengal," *Gender and History* v. 5, no. 2: 231–243; Kerber, *Women of the Republic*, p. 40; Beth Baron, "Mothers, Morality, and Nationalism in Pre-1919 Egypt, " in Rashid Khalidi, ed., *The Origins of Arab Nationalism* (New York: Columbia U. Press, 1991), pp. 271–288; Afsaneh Najmabadi, "Beloved and Mother: The Erotic Vatan [Homeland]: to Love, to Hold, and to Protect," paper delivered at the SSRC Conference, Cairo, May 28–30, 1993.

49. *Kalem* 11: 1, 30 Teşrin-i evvel 1324/12 November 1908, short months after the revolution, shows a noble figure of the army in a St. George–type scenario, facing off against a dragon, while the nubile young *Hürriyet* (Freedom), looking very much like a youthful Marianne in revolutionary cap, huddles under his arm.

50. *Kalem* 10: 1, 23 Teşrin-i evvel 1324/5 November 1908.

51. *Lak Lak* 12: 1, 24 Eylül 1325/7 October 1909. Similar images are found in the gazettes *Malum* and *Papagallo*.

52. Of course cartoon fashions are caricatures; images of "national" dress in cartoons often have little relationship to the standard conventions of fashion actually in place in a given country. Cartoons have traditionally taken the liberty of exaggerating dress to create types and suggest ideologies.

53. One could argue that the empire was feminized *because* it was weak, but the empire (called "the sick man of Europe" by Europeans since the nineteenth century), characterized as weak, was just as often gendered as male in Ottoman cartoons where, overall, many more cartoon characters were male than female.

54. Zehra Arat, "Turkish Women and the Republican Reconstruction of Tradition," pp. 57–80, in Fatma Müge Göçek and Shiva Balaghi, eds., *Reconstructing Gender in the Middle East: Tradition, Identity, and Power* (New York: Columbia University Press, 1994), points out the extent to which the Republican vision of women did and did not aim to elevate them above this condition of dependence and second-class-citizen status, after World War I. Despite the emphasis on the modern educated woman/mother in the rhetorics of the Young Turk and Atatürk regimes, the vision of a liberated and equal sister was still a long way off. That fact, in some ways, makes Fazlı's cartoon all the more striking.

55. Terms like *vatanperver* (patriot) could be gender-neutral, but when editorials directly addressed the public and wanted to point out their female audience, specific inclusionary terms of address, like *kadınlar* (women) were often added.

56. For a cartoon of the female as both consumer and patriot in the context of the boycott, see *Dalkavuk* 25: 1, 21 Şubat 1324/6 March 1909. She and her male companion are bypassing the establishment of a European shopkeeper even though he urges them to come in, because the boycott has "ended."

57. *Lak Lak* 13: 1, 1 Teşrin-i evvel 1325/14 October 1909.

58. Chatterjee, op. cit., p. 245, has argued that the "new" woman in India was demarcated both from the vulgar common woman and from the Europeanized collaborators: "It was precisely this degenerate condition [of the common woman void of superior moral sense] which nationalism claimed it would reform, and it was through these contrasts that the new woman of nationalist ideology was accorded a status of cultural superiority to the westernized women of the wealthy parvenu families spawned by the colonial connection as well as the common women of the lower classes. Attainment by her own efforts of a superior national culture was the mark of woman's newly acquired freedom." In the Otoman press, the citizen-patriot could be lower class, but was more often than not middle class. The vulgarization of the lower classes does not seem to be as extreme as Chatterjee suggests for India—perhaps because Ottoman satire often employed characters of the lower (agrarian or urban laboring) classes in the role of sister and brother sufferers from the effects of European imperialism and, hence, as fellow citizen-patriots. A fertile ground for further comparison and exploration of these ideas is Latin America (Brazil, for example), which was undergoing some of the same political, cultural, and economic changes as the Ottoman state (at about the same time), but where labor movements and labor consciousness were often much more highly developed than in Istanbul at the time of the revolution.

59. For analogies to the United States, see Kerber, *Women of the Republic*, pp. 69–136; and for the "better wives and mothers" of the Republican era in Turkey, see Arat, "Turkish Women," pp. 58–60.

60. This visual juxtaposition mirrors the juxtaposition of women to men in naming (identification), official documents, law, and literature, where women were commonly identified on the basis of their relationship to a man. Vir Bharat Talwar, "Feminist Consciousness in Women's Journals in Hindi: 1910–1920," in *Recasting Women*, p. 209, notes that an Indian gazette in 1919 introduced a book by a female author by noting whose wife she was. Such naming was also common practice of long duration in the Ottoman

empire, as elsewhere.

61. Much has been written on the mother-patriot, and the associations of repro-
duction with value, work, and civic duty. For some examples, see: Deborah
L. Rhode, ed., *Theoretical Perspectives on Sexual Difference* (New Haven:
Yale University Press, 1990); Fedwa Malti-Douglas, *Woman's Body,
Woman's Word: Gender and Discourse in Arabo-Islamic Writing* (Princeton:
Princeton University Press, 1991); Joan Wallach Scott, *Gender and the
Politics of History* (New York: Columbia University Press, 1988), pp.
93–112; Geraldine Heng and Janadas Devan, "State Fatherhood: The
Politics of Nationalism, Sexuality and Race in Singapore" (and other
entries), in Parker et. al., eds., *Nationalisms and Sexualities*, pp. 343–364.

62. *Kalem* 85: 5, 22 Nisan 1326/5 May 1910.

63. An interesting example of the conflation of female citizen-patriot with the
production of an army is found in Nira Yuval-Davis, "Front and Rear: The
Sexual Division of Labour in the Israeli Army," in Haleh Afshar, ed.,
Women, State and Ideology: Studies from Africa and Asia (London:
MacMillan Press, 1987), pp. 185–203, which illustrates how the liberating
image of female combatants in the Israeli army is firmly tied to the notions
of mother-patriots, women as comforters of men and producers of a new
generation of soldiers.

64. These women are an interesting combination of old and new associations.
Victoria Bonelle, "The Peasant Woman in Stalinist Political Art of the
1930s," *American Historical Review* 98, no. 1 (February 1993): 55–73,
points out the contradiction in the depiction of peasant women after the
Russian Revolution that makes them both heroic icons (the new peasant
woman), as workers and the backbone of the state, while continuing to asso-
ciate them with (old peasant woman) traits like: "fecundity and shrewdness
as well as ignorance, greed, and subordination to the patriarchal rural world"
(p. 55).

65. There is a certain irony in this cartoon, an irony that degenders the new generation in order to defend the imperilled nation.

66. Recent scholarship on women in Middle Eastern states has focused on
silence as a mode by which Islamic systems and androcentric historiography
have controlled women. See, for example, Farzaneh Milani, *Veils and
Words: The Emerging Voices of Iranian Women Writers* (Syracuse: Syracuse
University Press, 1992); and Leila Ahmed, *Women and Gender in Islam*
(New Haven: Yale University Press, 1992), p. 61. These authors present
women who have and have not been silenced. In the case of the Ottoman
press (Istanbul, in 1908, was and still is an Islamic society) we find the old
nag archetype as a traditional symbol of the unsilenced woman—of the

woman who, indeed, represents the voice of public anxiety, concern, and irony.

67. The literal meaning of Büyük Hanım is "Big" Lady, and sometimes the satirists drew her as big, playing with the ambiguity of the term; but the conventional use suggests advanced age, a term of respect, or grandma. The gazette *Dalkavuk* (September 1908–March 1909) contains various humorous dialogues between "Büyük Hanım" and others including "Kızım" (meaning "my daughter" although it can be applied to any young woman). Büyük Hanım can also be found in *Boşboğaz* 13: 2, 8 Eylül 1324/21 September 1908. A similar figure is "Hanım Nene" (mother, nurse, wet-nurse) in *İncili Çavuş* 14: 4, 23 Eylül 1324/6 October 1908. See also *Lak Lak* 3: 3, 23 Temmuz 1325/5 August 1909, for a "woman in the street" cartoon.

68. *Geveze* was published by Kirkor Faik between fall of 1908 and spring of 1909 (until shortly after the abortive Ottoman counter-revolution). Its successor, *Yeni Geveze* (New Blabbermouth), published 1910–1912, contains a spectacular array of Ottoman cartooning styles.

69. *Hande* 1: 34, 22 Mart 1326/4 April 1910. The image of the gossiping woman appears here and there in the press, as for example in the "national novel/story" (*milli roman*) entitled "Gossipy Women" (*Dedikoducu Kadınlar*), published in *Cingöz* 1: 2, 29 Ağustos 1324/11 September 1908.

70. *Cadaloz* was published for five months, in 1910, by Nureddin Rüşdi, Haydar Rüşdi, and Hüseyin Nazmi. It contains some of the revolutionary period's most biting satire.

71. Cadaloz means spiteful or vindictive, or (embodied) it means a spiteful old hag. The gender of Cadaloz seems to be purposefully ambivalent; in some cartoons "she" looks more like a woman and, in others, more like a man.

72. As argued in another context for the women of the Ottoman harem in Leslie Peirce, *The Imperial Harem: Women and Sovereignty in the Ottoman Empire* (Oxford: Oxford University Press, 1993), pp. 20–23, 91–112.

73. Chatterjee, op. cit., p. 244, has noted the association of loudness and quarrelsomeness with the "common" woman, lower-class female characters who inhabit nineteenth-century literature: maidservants, washerwomen, barbers, peddlers, procuresses, prostitutes. There are some similarities here to the Ottoman old nag, who is usually dressed and framed as a member of the lower or middle classes, ordinarily not a member of the elite classes.

74. *Cadaloz* 13: 4, 3 Mayis 1327/16 May 1911.

75. *Kalem* 109: 10, 6 Kanun-ı sani, 1326/January 19, 1911. The French caption, as in many bilingual cartoons, does not exactly match the Ottoman caption. For a 1909 image of the fashionable woman and ice-skating in the European

context, see Max von Boehn and Oskar Fischel, *Modes and Manners of the Nineteenth Century as Represented in the Pictures and Engravings of the Time* (London: J. M. Dent and Co., 1909), v. 3, *1843–1875*, p. 114.

76. Pierre Teilhard de Chardin, *Letters from Egypt 1905–1908* (New York: Herder and Herder, 1965), p. 246, notes that roller skating was also "all the rage" in Cairo in 1908.

77. *Kalem* 53: 15, 3 Eylül 1325/16 September 1909.

78. There are many Ottoman cartoons on skating. The falls associated with skating made it an obvious target of humor but it was also satirized, as here, more pointedly to critique the effects of Western cultural influences.

79. European women and those who imitated their free behavior in public were cause for various types of criticism and concern. Mrs. De Leon, in a chapter contributed to Edwin de Leon's *Thirty Years of My Life On Three Continents* (London: Ward and Donwey, 1890), v. 2, pp. 217–218, notes that one of the Egyptian Princesses remarked on how foreign women were riding spirited horses and "conversing with men in public with uncovered faces." For a variety of treatments of the public vs. private sphere dichotomy in the analysis of women's behavior and social convention, see Nikki Keddie and Beth Baron, eds., *Women in Middle Eastern History: Shifting Boundaries in Sex and Gender* (New Haven: Yale University Press, 1991).

80. The cinema was another new development imported from Europe. *Kalem* 100: 11, 21 Teşrin-i evvel 1326/4 December 1910, advertised an Ottoman "Cinema Orientaux," located at 164 Grand Rue de Péra in Istanbul in 1910. The films would show "sensational events, the Portuguese revolution, William II at Brussels, art films."

81. Emine Tugay, *Three Centuries: Family Chronicles of Turkey and Egypt* (London: Oxford University Press, 1963), pp. 176–277. The author was a member of the Khedival family living in Izmir and her father was an important member of the Ottoman elite who had supported the cinema–skating rink proposal. To circumvent public criticism while seeing that the show went on, Tugay's mother bought up all the tickets for the first ladies' performance. Emine and her brothers received private skating lessons at home from the rink's owner. After her father's term of office, the concession for the rink and cinema was not renewed.

82. *Diken* published by Sedat Simavi, began publication in November 1918 and ended in 1920. See for example, *Diken* 23: 8–9, 18 Eylül 1335/1 October 1919, for the mascot old nag juxtaposed to a very chic *alafranga* woman with parasol, and for the old nag (called *cadi*, witch or hag) scolding the *alafranga* woman in the street while male passers-by snicker. There are various juxtapositions of the old nag and the *alafranga* woman throughout

Diken, mostly for social satirical purposes.

83. R. Radhakrishnan, "Nationalism, Gender, and the Narrative of Identity, " in Parker, *Nationalisms and Sexualities*, pp. 84–85, has suggested that the colonial context trapped Indian nationalism into a dichotomous rhetoric of interior and exterior, thus defining the limits of the symbolic representation of women. He notes: "The particular instance of Indian nationalism makes use of the inner/outer distinction as a way of selectively coping with the West, and it is not coincidental that the women's question is very much part of this dichotomous adjustment. Here again, by mobilizing the inner/outer distinction against the 'outerness' of the West, nationalist rhetoric makes 'woman' the pure and ahistorical signifier of 'interiority'. In the fight against the enemy from the outside, something within gets even more repressed and 'woman' becomes the mute but necessary allegorical ground for the transactions of nationalist history." The Ottoman empire was likewise faced with the problem of defining its identity in contrast to Europe, although in the Ottoman case "colonization" was economic and cultural. Woman as a pure and ahistorical signifier of interiority, in the Ottoman press, was only one option; the "outerness" or "otherness" of the West was also projected *onto* Ottoman woman. Nor were cartoon Ottoman women *only* mute or allegorical. The old nag, in particular, is distinguished as singularly not mute; she is also freed from the position of being under male guidance which so often characterizes her citizen-patriot cartoon sisters.

84. On the patriarchal bargain see Deniz Kandiyoti, "Islam and Patriarchy: A Comparative Perspective," in Keddie and Baron, eds., *Women in Middle Eastern History*, pp. 23–44. The model of the patriarchal bargain de-emphasizes patriarchy as monolithic and focuses instead on analyzing women's strategies for dealing with male dominance.

Political Culture in the
Iranian Revolution of 1906 and
The Cartoons of *Kashkul*

SHIVA BALAGHI

The relationship between iconography and politics offers the historian an interesting lens through which to examine shifts in political practices. Throughout the history of Iran, visual representations have been used to depict the political authority of the ruler. The walls of Persepolis depict peoples from around the Persian Empire bearing tribute and paying homage to the Achaemenid kings. Faces of kings have adorned coins. Miniatures in the illuminated manuscripts of the *Shahnameh* offer images of imperial power, both real and mythic. Concomitantly, the often highly visual imagery of panegyric poetry has served to glorify countless monarchs. During the Constitutional Revolution of 1906–1911, iconography once again played a part in the articulation of political power in Iran. While the use of iconography during the Constitutional Revolution may have drawn on these past traditions of politicized cultural representation, I suggest that there were also digressions from past political practices that reflect important aspects of the revolutionary culture of the Constitutional period. A close examination of some political cartoons which were printed in the newspaper *Kashkul* can help to illustrate the changing tropes of representations of the Iranian body politic and the changing patterns of political practices.[1]

The impact of print on Iranian cultural production has held a particular fascination for me. The advent of print journalism and changes in the production of books had a vast influence on Iranian cultural, intellectual, and political history. The printing press and lithography forged a peculiar relationship between the realms of technology, politics, and culture—a historical convergence which has shaped the history of Qajar Iran in ways that remain largely understudied and unexamined by the historians.[2] While some have remarked on the flow of publication that followed the Constitutional Revolution, few have seriously considered the importance of print culture in shaping the Revolution itself. The political cartoons which I examine were published in the year 1907, while the Revolution was still underway. As such, they offer a compelling window into the Revolution during a critical time—when its future was unclear, its factions were still being fomented, its philosophies were still being debated, and its institutions were still being shaped.

A brief review of the key events of the Constitutional Revolution through 1907 will help delineate the context within which these cartoons were drawn and elucidate the ways in which the "reading" of political cartoons reveals some of the undercurrents of the revolutionary period. The event which sparked the Revolution occurred in December 1905, when the governor of Tehran ordered some sugar merchants bastinadoed for refusing to lower their prices. A group of merchants, tradesmen, and mullahs took sanctuary (*bast*) in a mosque in Tehran. Government officials dispersed the group who then took refuge at the shrine of 'Abd al-'Azim south of Tehran. They were joined by some 2000 people and remained at the shrine for 25 days. In January 1906, the Shah agreed to the group's demand to form an *'adalatkhanah* (house of justice) and to dismiss the governor of Tehran. Neither the protesters nor the Shah, however, clearly defined the purpose or the nature of this house of justice, which remained a theoretical and amorphous entity whose specific nature and purpose remained undefined at this point. The Shah took no measures to seriously implement his promised *'adalatkhanah* and discontent continued to simmer. Finally, in a confrontation between some clergy and their followers, a young *sayyid* was killed.

This led to another mass protest including mullahs, merchants, and tradesmen in July 1906. Between 12,000 and 14,000 protesters took refuge in the British legation. The protesters of this second *bast* demanded the formation of a *majlis*, a parliament, to which the Shah finally agreed.[3] Though Muzaffar al-Din Shah agreed to the formation of a national assembly in a decree issued on August 5, 1906, the declaration was vague and did not clearly discuss the nature of the assembly or the way it would be implemented. As Nader Sohrabi has argued, "the wording of the decree. . . likened the National Consultative Assembly to an advisory panel of reform rather than a legislative assembly. Furthermore, it failed to mention the word 'constitution.'"[4] The first *majlis* convened in October 1906 and formed a committee, which set about writing a Fundamental Law, using a translation of the Belgian Constitution as their legislative model. The ailing Shah signed the law in December of 1906, just days before he died. His successor, Muhammad 'Ali Shah, signed the Supplementary Fundamental Law in October of 1907. "These two documents . . . formed the core of the Iranian constitution until 1979."[5]

Though he had come to some agreement with the constitutionalists, Muhammad 'Ali Shah hoped to squelch the movement. To that effect, he appointed the conservative (and much disliked) Amin as-Sultan to the premiership. Despite the Shah's hopes that he would dismiss the *majlis*, however, Amin as-Sultan tried to forge a compromise between the royal camp and the conservative parliamentarians. This move proved to be unpopular all around and Amin as-Sultan was assassinated on August 31, 1907.[6] On the very same day, the Anglo-Russian Convention partitioning Iran into spheres of influence was signed.[7] Though the assassination of his premier temporarily thwarted his plans to destroy the *majlis*, Muhammad 'Ali Shah remained ill disposed towards the concept of constitutional monarchy and the *majlis*.[8]

It is important to study the cartoons published in *Kashkul* in the year 1907 with an awareness of the historical landscape within which they were drawn. The internal political power struggle between the constitutionalists and the monarchy was unresolved. The framework of the constitution was still being debated by the parliamentarians. The parameters of constitutional monarchy were undefined and vague, even though a parliament was in existence. What did a constitutional monarchy entail in the Iranian context? How would an essentially secular idea, constitutionalism, be reconciled with Iran's Shi'i religion? What, in specific terms, would be the nature of the political relationship between the monarchy and the parliament? The ideological boundaries and institutional representations of constitutionalism were still being contested. By 1907, the Revolution was well underway, but its fate remained very much unsettled and unsure. Indeed, the tenuous nature of the Revolution is reflected in some of the cartoons of *Kashkul*. This is a body of cultural representation which lacks the grand solidity of the palaces of Persepolis; these cartoons reflect an underlying tension, instability, and uncertainty.[9] These cartoons were not meant to mummify pre-existing political orders; rather, they were a venue for questioning, for postulating, and for experimenting with new forms of political order.[10]

I am suggesting that the power of symbolism, which was a pre-existing feature of Iranian politics, offered the revolutionaries an important vehicle for articulating new ideas about politics. They did not, however, simply reflect the state of affairs as they were but offered the intellectuals a way to work through some of the ambiguity that was inherent in the Revolution. For the historian of Qajar Iran, then, these cartoons offer a glimpse into the very process of transformation; these are visual representations of change, not a reification of a static political order. By studying them, we might get a better sense of how some Iranian intellectuals living amidst the Revolution understood (and contributed to) the changes taking place. These cartoons, then, not only captured the nature of the revolutionary transformations taking place, they were a potentially transformative political medium in and of themselves.[11]

The political cartoons that appeared in the lithographed pages of *Kashkul* differed from other symbolic representations of political power in other respects as well. The circulation of a newspaper is broader, and access to its messages more widely possible, than inscriptions on monuments or miniatures of illuminated manuscripts. When thinking of the Arabo- Persian word for print (*nashar*, lit. to spread), one gets a sense of the primary importance of print as a means of the distribution of ideas. In previous studies, I have focused attention on matters of circulation of printed materials and the positionality of the audience in print culture.[12] The potential for duplication and circulation of ideas that the printing press permitted expanded the public sphere; indeed some have argued that print culture in effect created the public sphere. The boundaries demarcating those who were part of the public and those who were not has been determined by access to writing and reading printed material.[13]

But political cartoons that appeared in newspapers in Qajar Iran may well have expanded the boundaries of print culture beyond those of literacy alone. They translated the political messages of the newspapers for those who could not read. Indeed, in the very first issue of *Kashkul,* its editor, Majd al-Islam Kirmani clearly stated that by creating a newspaper that focused primarily on cartoons (for he was already the editor of another newspaper which included mainly written articles), he intended to create representations of events and people as a means to convey messages to the Iranian people.[14] Because of the possibility of wider dissemination, then, the images embedded in the political cartoons of *Kashkul* have a different kind of political currency than previous forms of political symbolism.[15]

In her analysis of the symbolic forms of political practice during the French Revolution of 1789, Lynn Hunt has argued that the authors of that revolution's iconography borrowed aspects of popular culture, politicized them, and redistributed them to the people. In so doing, the French revolutionaries were able to embody the legitimacy of "the people" in their political rhetoric. The intellectuals and politicians involved in these acts of symbolic appropriation were thereby able to place themselves in an important mediatory position between the realms of popular culture and revolutionary politics.[16] In his observations on the increasing politicization of popular culture in early modern Europe, the historian Peter Burke argued that this process was intrinsically connected to the rise of nationalism. Increasingly, intellectuals came to borrow their symbols not just from the elitist intellectual movements but from the ritualistic practices of popular culture, only to recirculate them to the people in politicized and increasingly nationalized forms.[17] The editor of *Kashkul* argued that newspapers were the "truth-revealing mirror of the nation."[18] As such, the editors of the newspapers (and the artists who drew the political cartoons) effectively assumed the authorship of the national images that were central to the articulation of the political messages of the Constitutional Revolution. Therein lies one of the major points of departure from previous symbolic forms of political practices common in Iran—no longer did the monarchy monopolize authorship over the articulation and use of political symbolism. The primary function of this form of cultural production was not simply to reinforce the relationship between the ruler (the

Figure 1

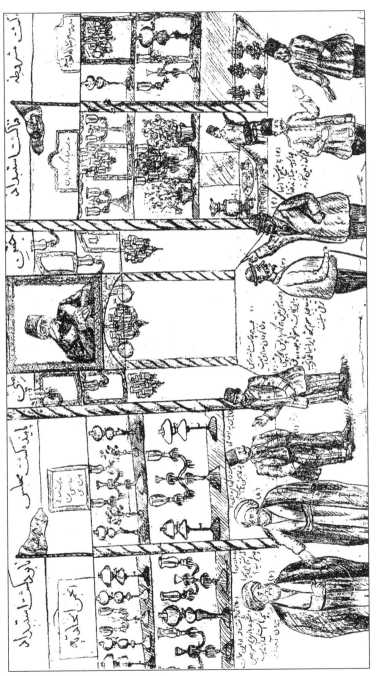

Figure 2

king) and the ruled (the people). The shifting power relations of the time were reflected in this new cultural venue. The printing press was instrumental in challenging the monopoly of the court over politicized cultural production. In the pages of *Kashkul,* Majd al-Islam,[19] as the editor, and Mirza 'Ali, as the cartoonist, were interpreting ongoing political currents, pointing to problems, offering social criticism, educating and informing the people, cautioning the politicians—all the while constructing new tropes of nationhood which they deemed appropriate for the revolutionary Iranian body politic. In effect, "reading" these cartoons nearly a century later involves decoding not just the symbols they used, but the process of symbolism they deployed—and discerning the correlative institutionalization of the forms of government which was their concern. By so doing, we may begin to understand the ways in which government itself came to have new meanings in Iran during the Constitutional Revolution.

Raymond Williams suggested that the reproduction of images in the European context was directly connected to the extension of trade and empire, arguing, ". . . the use of the reproducible image of authority became and has remained very important."[20] The process of representing authority in the cultural domain was significant in the Iranian context, as well, especially when the boundaries of political authority were highly contested. It is important to note that the process of imaging, of creating representations of Iran through cartoons, was a conscious one. As I have noted, Majd al-Islam specifically chose cartoons as a medium for representing issues and events that he deemed important for the Iranian people. But Majd al-Islam and Mirza 'Ali's understanding of the process of representation and its importance in Iranian nationalism was conveyed in some of the cartoons of *Kashkul,* as well. They were aware that they competed with other forces for the authorship of the allegories of the Iranian nation.[21] They seemed cognizant of the use of representation by the European powers and by the Iranian monarchy alike. Here, they deployed satire in order to undermine and question other attempts to define the Iranian nation.

In one cartoon, the idea of exhibitions is parodied (see fig. 1). The nineteenth century was a time when the world-as-exhibition played an important part in the construction of colonial power.[22] In this cartoon, we see a satirical twist on the idea of Iran at the exhibition.[23] The caption tells us this Exposition features displays of Iranian industry and trade. Featured booths include a *kaleh pazi* and a *dizi pazi*. These are both traditional Iranian foods that lower-class people eat. The first booth features a pot of broth made from sheeps' heads and the cooked sheeps' heads arranged on a tray. A bearded man wearing traditional Iranian clothes mans the booth and several men are shown sitting on the floor of the booth, eating away. The next booth is selling *dizi*, a popular dish in Iran. In the street, we see a man peddling sweet beets. There are several stray dogs begging for food. One man sits in the street, smoking a pipe (which may well be filled with opium). The scene is generally a dismal one, focusing on the lifestyle of the urban poor, the lower classes. It seems to satirize the attempts to represent Iran in the industrial exhibitions, as it underlines the disparity between the poverty of the people and the desire of the government to industrialize Iran. It seems to critique modes of representation which belie the economic hardships and "traditional" lifestyles of the Iranian people.

Another cartoon which indicates that the editor and cartoonist of *Kashkul* were aware of alternative venues of representation of the Iranian nation appears in an issue published on August 10, 1907—a time that was pregnant with political turmoil in Iran (see fig. 2).[24] This full-page cartoon features a variety of powers that were interested in the representation of the Iranian nation. Its central focal point is a portrait of Muzaffar al-Din Shah Qajar with his characteristically sleepy eyes. His arms are folded in front of him, and he is wearing the regal costume of the king. The picture sits amidst what appears to be the architectural equivalent of the court and its institutions, featuring various rooms that are filled with lamps, mirrors, plates of sweets and flowers—suggesting a festival is taking place. There are two flags which bear the insignia of the court, the lion and the sun. Amongst the institutions that are named are the Dar al-Fanun, the school which was instrumental to the court's attempt to establish a secular educational system. There are banners flanking the Shah's portrait which celebrate constitutionalism and the parliament and announce the end of oppression. One sign announces a national festival. Beneath this scene, there are four pairs of men speaking who represent the different constituencies involved in Iranian politics at the time. One pair features two mullahs who are wondering why students are participating in the national festival. The next pair of commentators are dressed in westernized clothing and ostensibly represent the educated technocrats. They claim that all there is (that benefits the nation) stems from the students of the schools. Another pair are clearly Europeans, who comment that no such festival has even been seen in Paris; these elaborate festivals surely indicate that the Iranians are pursuing progress. The final pair are dressed in official governmental attire; their discussion is in the form of an idiomatic expression exclaiming that these people are striding atop four horses and trying not to fall to the ground. This cartoon would seem to suggest a contest over the use of festivals, symbols, and institutions in order to affect the shape and character of the Iranian nation. It strongly suggests that the symbolic power of representation was a site of competition amongst different factions engaged in the Iranian political system at the time. The unresolved nature of the debate over the right to speak for the nation and to define its constituency is reflected in the cartoon. The tenor of the cartoon evokes a cacophony of voices with a stake in defining the fate of the Iranian nation at this juncture of the Revolution.

Given that the Constitutional Revolution had not yet coalesced and remained incomplete, it would seem that part of the mission of the cartoons of *Kashkul* was to help give form and direction to the undercurrent of chaos that was endemic to revolutionary politics. The cartoons illustrate the cultural hybridity which marked so much of Qajar Iran's cultural production.[25] Though it is clear that the cartoonist and the editor of *Kashkul* were aware of political trends in Europe and their influence on the Iranian political scene, they were equally cognizant of Iran's history and its contemporary political circumstances. They borrowed from internal and imported practices and tropes in order to create symbols and political messages that were appropriate to the specific circumstances of the Constitutional Revolution. The process of cultural adaptation to changing political circumstances was not one of wholesale Westernization, even if the political tropes of "the West" were familiar to the players of the Constitutional period. The Iranian experiment with modernity, as expressed in the cartoons of *Kashkul*, was much more nuanced than that.

The complicated process of cultural translation that was taking place within the cartoons of *Kashkul* can be better understood by examining one particular cartoon which stands out as a stunning representation of the political struggles of these times. It was published in the issue appearing on June 8, 1907.[26] The cartoon blends features of Iranian culture with ones borrowed from Europe; it sets forth a powerful image of the Iranian nation, even as it underlines the uncertainty of the political situation (see fig. 3).

Figure 3

The cartoon features a virile, muscular man who is dressed in garb befitting an Iranian wrestler; he wears a thick moustache, curled up at the ends in the fashion favored in the Qajar period. His muscles are clearly delineated through his athletic costume. The word *millat* (nation) is embellished on his belt. He stands atop a stylized globe, marked with the word *vatan* (country). The nation is holding a scale. One part of the scale is inscribed with the word *saltanat* (monarchy); the other part with the word *majlis* (parliament). A group of jesters are throwing rocks onto the scale trying to tip the balance. In the background, we see some peasants and mullahs looking on mockingly.

The title of this cartoon is "The Constitutional Monarchy of Iran." The political dilemma so evocatively captured by the cartoonist Mirza 'Ali is further elaborated on in the article which accompanies the cartoon. It suggests that "we, the Iranian nation" need to maintain a balance between both the monarchy and the parliament. In order to pass effective laws, enact these laws, and run an effective government, both the monarchy and the parliament are necessary. There are those who may try "to throw stones" and tip the balance between the two, or who may argue that one of these institutions is no longer essential. The Iranian nation must resist "the trickery of the devil" who wants the country to lose its balance and fall to ruination. Maintaining a balance between the monarchy and the parliament, then, was paramount to the survival of Iran—and the political agent charged with keeping these two forces in their proper place was the Iranian nation.

Interestingly, the Iranian nation as depicted in this cartoon is one that is set apart from important constituencies—the peasantry and the clergy. Their relationship to the institutional representation of governmental power (the monarchy and the parliament) and to the Iranian nation is ambiguous and almost marginal. Their only form of participation in this interaction between the Iranian nation and its political system is to stand in the margins, mockingly observing the political struggle taking place. The Iranian nation is represented as a strong man, one dressed in the garb of a wrestler—a modern day *pahlavan* of sorts. But the cartoon offers no clues as to which class, which group of people, compose this nation. The caption reinforces this dichotomous representation of the Iranian nation—as being powerful and yet remaining largely undefined in specific terms. While they are cautioned about the devil's desire to tip the balance of power of the new Constitutional Monarchy, little specific discussion takes place about how these new political machinations, these systems of checks and balances are to take place. The specific point of entry into the political system of the Iranian nation, the mechanisms by which they are to safeguard the balance of power, remains altogether unclear. Therefore, it can be argued, even as the cartoon represents the Iranian nation in *pahlavan*-esque dimensions, it does not offer any practical means by which this powerful nation can actually influence the political system effectively. In this case, there seems to be an unreconciled disparity between form and reality, between theory and practice.

Another cartoon which appeared in *Kashkul,* again drawn by Mirza 'Ali, offers yet another depiction of the Iranian nation (see fig. 4). The title of this cartoon is "The current political situation in Iran," and it appears in an issue of *Kashkul* printed in September of 1907.[27] In the middle of the full page cartoon, we see a boiling pot filled with babies. Some of the babies are crying out; others are smiling innocently. One baby crawls playfully on the ground in front of the pot. To the right of the pot, we see a tiger in pursuit of its prey. To the left of the pot, we see a growling bear emerging from the woods. Above the boiling pot, we see a bird which has swooped down and taken a baby into its beak. In the upper corner, we see a man dressed in a European style suit running from the scene, and saying that he is leaving and the situation seems very bleak. This representation of the Iranian nation stands in sharp contrast to the previous cartoon discussed. Here, the cartoonist Mirza 'Ali turns his attention to the imperial interest in Iran. The tiger represents British India; the bear represents Russia. This depiction of the Iranian nation renders it as helpless and powerless.

An editorial entitled "The national movement in defense of the country," printed in the same issue as this cartoon, may help us to decipher the particular context in which this cartoon was drawn. In the page-long article, the editors complain about the high level of taxation. These taxes, it is argued, are ostensibly collected in order to ward off an Ottoman threat to Urumia. Indeed, the editor claims, the people of Iran pay taxes in order to ensure the security of the nation from both internal and external forces. Why should they continue to pay such high prices when there is still not adequate security and protection? If the taxes were going to pay for guns and munitions, the people would gladly oblige, but this is not the case. People are complaining to the editors of *Kashkul*, because they do not want their taxes to go to paying for "gambling in the night and Russian horses and dolls."[28] The editors write that they cannot give the people any assurances unless the *majlis* intervenes directly in this matter.[29]

The images of the Iranian nation as represented in the second cartoon and its auxiliary article stand in sharp contrast to the earlier cartoon which I discussed. Previously, the Iranian nation had been presented as a strong man who stood at the nexus of political power. In this cartoon, the Iranian nation is represented as babies, helpless and vulnerable to domestic and foreign enemies. According to the editorial preceding the cartoon, when faced with internal corruption, the Iranian people were left feeling vulnerable and frustrated. Their only recourse was to go to the offices of *Kashkul* in search of answers. It was the editors of the newspaper who called for the Parliament to act in order to protect the rights of the people (*mardum*). In neither the editorial nor the cartoon do we find depictions of an Iranian nation that has political power. In both cases, their connection to the parliament seems unclear. In the cartoon, the character dressed in a suit (ostensibly the Westernized elite) is running away. In the editorial, the complaints are carried to the offices of newspapers rather than directly to the *majlis*, the representative assembly. Constitutional government, that is a political mechanism which reflects the will of the people, seems illusive at best. Importantly, in this cartoon it remains unclear who the bird is meant to represent; the salvation of the Iranian people, the bird that will carry them from the burning fires to a safe haven, remains an unknown entity at this political juncture.

If these cartoons leave the relationship of the Iranian nation vis-ĵ-vis the constitutional government vague and indeterminate, other cartoons suggest ways in which people can help to bolster the new national institutions. The purpose of these cartoons seems to be to educate the people about the virtues of these institutions and to garner their support for them. The very first issue of *Kashkul*, for example, deals with the national bank. Its last page shows the national bank which boasts the insignia of the lion and the sun. There is a huge line of people standing in line to enter the bank. The Iranians represent a wide cross-section of people, including

Figure 4

clergy, peasants, tribal men, westernized members of the upper classes, and even women (though they are heavily veiled). The women are standing to the side of the crowd. One wonders whether they too should be joining the crowd and giving their money to the bank; the other woman responds that they should make deposits into the bank as well in hopes that in the coming year things will improve.[30] A second cartoon entitled "the soldiers of the nation" shows rows of orderly soldiers, wearing new uniforms, bearing arms, and standing at attention. An officer asks the soldiers if they know what their duty is. The soldiers answer that they are commissioned on behalf of the entire nation to sacrifice their lives in order to protect the country.[31] These two cartoons suggest that people can serve the Iranian nation, which is suffering from internal and external pressures, in direct ways—by joining the army and depositing their cash into the national bank. Here, the role of the Iranian people in the struggle for constitutionalism is more clear—by contributing their bodies and their income to bolster the burgeoning national institutions. While the cartoons that I discussed earlier (figs. 3 and 4) fail to define the place of the Iranian nation in the constitutional crisis by not delineating the means by which they can have a direct influence over the political machinations of the constitutional monarchy, here we see a more direct means of participation for the people (*mardum*) as a nation (*millat*). The role designated to the people of Iran in these cartoons does not include a direct voice in shaping the contours of constitutionalism and nationalism in Iran during the pivotal year of 1907.

The above discussion of political cartoons in part demonstrates the usefulness of print culture as a venue through which to study the history of modern Iran. Though we may be mindful of the unfinished business of modernity in Iran, as historians, we seem hesitant to relate the same ambiguity and incompleteness when we write history. Or, perhaps I should say, the ambiguity of history, "the fragments of history" (to use Gyanendra Pandey's phrase) have yet to be embraced as valid and important historical subjects by those working on Iranian history.[32] The texture of our histories should reflect to some degree the contested nature of many of the subjects we write about. Studying the political cartoons of the Constitutional Revolution while the Revolution was still in progress offers us the opportunity to write the history of the revolutionary process, along with the commensurate instabilities inherent in that process.

As Robert Darnton has pointed out, there is a need to delve more deeply into "the social and cultural history of communication by print."[33] There is still much work to be done before the complete importance of print culture in the Qajar era can be appreciated. The study of print culture need not limit itself to the examination of books that are within the purview of "high culture." Persian presses in the nineteenth century in Tehran and the provinces, in Istanbul and Cairo, in Bombay and Lucknow produced pieces that belonged to the realm of popular culture as well. Nor should it be assumed that access to printed matter was limited to the literate alone. The cartoons of *Kashkul* and other newspapers conveyed their messages through parody and satire to the illiterate as well. If the cartoons were, indeed, the "mirrors of the nation," what I have been suggesting is that the mirror reflected the anxiety and uncertainty of the political crisis of Iran in 1907, when "the conflict between King and Parliament was at its height."[34] The pomposity of the national festivals of the monarchy, the fledgling national institutions, the unclear relationship of the monarch and the parliament were among the subjects of these cartoons. The struggle to represent and control the place of the Iranian nation within this constitutional struggle was also reflected in the crudely sketched cartoons of *Kashkul.*

What is of special interest is that the cartoons were unable, ultimately, to define the constituents of the Iranian nation (*millat*) or to carve out a role in the articulation of constitutionalism for it. The source of the nation's power and its agency within the constitutional movement was not fleshed out, not sufficiently mapped out. Only when illustrating the Iranian people (*mardum*) do the cartoons reflect a specific membership, and the political role of this people is to support the national institutions, by giving their money to the national banks and their young men to the national army. The iconography of the cartoons in *Kashkul* left the linkage between the Iranian people and the Iranian nation unresolved, an important shortcoming which at least in part explains the failure of the cartoons to become a more effective revolutionary tool. Even when the Iranian nation was represented as a strong figure, the specific source of its political power was not articulated. Furthermore, the iconography of these cartoons produced no Mariannes or John Bulls, no enduring symbols of liberty or national power that gripped the popular imagination.[35] Their primary function was perhaps to inform—those who lived in 1907 and those of us studying the history of that period—of a view of events that is not necessarily to be found in the transcripts of the parliamentary debates, the official histories produced by the Qajar state presses, or the diplomatic records of the colonial powers. They lend more texture to our reading of a crucial time in modern Iranian history, even if we can never fully appreciate what the eyes of an Iranian seeing these cartoons in 1907 might have discerned in their parodies.

Notes

1. The newspaper appears as entry #168 in H. L. Rabino's handlist. See H. L. Rabino, *Surat-i Jarayid-i Iran va Jarayid-i ke dar Kharij-i Iran be Zaban-i Farsi Tab' Shudah Ast* (Rasht, 1329); E. G. Browne, *The Press and Poetry of Modern Persia* (Los Angeles: Kalimat Press, 1983, originally published in 1914), p. 127; Mohammad Sadr-Hashemi, *Tarikh-i Jarayid va Majallat-i Iran* (Isfahan, 1327), v. 4, pp. 135–137.

2. Here, I am not arguing that the printing press was introduced into Iran during the reign of the Qajars. Indeed, as E. G. Browne wrote, the Armenians had established a printing press at Julfa in Isfahan as early as 1650. What I am arguing, however, is that the political importance of the printing press came to full fruition in the Qajar era. See E. G. Browne, "The Persian Press and Persian Journalism," text of lecture delivered to the Persia Society, May 23, 1913.

3. For a summary of the political history of the period, see Nikki Keddie and Mehrdad Amanat, "Iran Under the Later Qajars, 1848–1922," *The Cambridge History of Iran*, v. 7 (Cambridge: Cambridge University Press, 1991): 174–211. See also Mangol Bayat, *Iran's First Revolution* (N.Y.: Oxford University Press, 1991).

4. Nader Sohrabi, "Historicizing Revolutions: Constitutional Revolutions in the Ottoman Empire, Iran, and Russia, 1905–1908," *American Journal of Sociology*, Volume 100, no. 6 (May 1995): 1396.

5. Keddie and Amanat, "Iran Under the Late Qajars," p. 203.

6. Nikki Keddie, "The Assassination of Amin As-Sultan (Atabak-i A'zam) 31 August 1907," in *Iran and Islam: in Memory of Vladimir Minorsky*, ed. C. E. Bosworth (Edinburgh: University of Edinburgh Press, 1971): 315–30.

7. S. Balaghi, "The Iconography of Power: The Political Cartoons of *Kashkul* and the Anglo-Russian Convention of 1907," forthcoming.

8. In June of 1908, Muhammad 'Ali Shah's troops stormed the *majlis*. The following summer, the counter-revolution was thwarted and the parliament was reconvened.

9. In his discussion of the political crisis of representation which surrounded the French Revolution, Antoine de Baecque suggests that one of the chief uses of allegorical representation during the French Revolution was to help sift through the "historical fracture" produced by revolutionary transformations. De Baecque argues that allegory served to describe events, to lend those descriptions "imaginative resonance," and to provide a means of understanding, "a structure of knowledge for perceiving the events." Antoine de Baecque, "The Allegorical Image of France, 1750–1800: A Political Crisis of Representation," *Representations* 47 (1994): 111–137. Interestingly, Brummett finds a similar anxiety reflected in cartoons produced in Turkey in 1908 during that country's constitutional revolution. See Palmira Brummett, "Dogs, Women, Cholera, and Other Menaces in the Streets: Cartoon Satire in the Ottoman Revolutionary Press, 1908–1911," *International Journal of Middle East Studies* 27 (1995): 433–460.

10. In his study of the famous British cartoonist Hogarth, Marcus Wood suggests that Hogarth was able to blend elements of satire and representation from the tradition of illuminated manuscripts, carvings, and etchings on buildings with aspects of British folk culture in order to produce caricatures that linked British popular culture with the politics of the times. The growth of the print trade in late eighteenth-century England, Wood argues, brought about the possible fusion of social satire and political propoganda in a way that enmeshed folk culture with cultural elements of the church, the court, and the government. Marcus Wood, *Radical Satire and Print Culture, 1790–1822* (Oxford: Clarendon Press, 1994).

11. For an important discussion of the satirical rhetorical devices deployed by other newspapers being published roughly at the same time as *Kashkul* see Janet Afary, "Journalism, Satire, and Revolution: Exposing the Conservative Clerics, Denouncing the Western Powers," in *The Iranian Constitutional Revolution, 1906–1911* (N.Y.: Columbia University Press, 1996): 116–142.

12. S. Balaghi, "The Iranian as Spectator and Spectacle: Theater and Nationalism in Nineteenth Century Iran," in *Social Constructions of Nationalism in the Middle East*, ed. F. Müge Göçek, forthcoming; S. Balaghi, "The Shift from the Manuscript to the Printed Book in Qajar Iran," working paper.

13. The effective argument is made in Roger Chartier, *The Cultural Origins of the French Revolution* (Durham: Duke University Press, 1991).

14. See *Kashkul* year 1, no. 1 (March 30, 1907), p. 1.

15. For a discussion of the Ottoman press as a revolutionary agent, see Bernard Lewis, "New Media: The Press," in *The Emergence of Modern Turkey* (Oxford: Oxford University Press, 1968): 146–150. Zachary Lockman has shown the importance of print culture in shaping notions of the working class as an integral component of Egyptian nationalism, see "Imagining the Working Class: Culture, Nationalism, and Class Formation in Egypt, 1899–1914," *Poetics Today* 15 (1994): 157–190. Albert Hourani and Ami Ayalon offer an analysis of the historical context of the political role of Arab journalism: see Albert Hourani, *Arabic Thought in the Liberal Age, 1798–1939* (Cambridge: Cambridge University Press, 1983); Ami Ayalon, "*Sihafa*: The Arab Experiment in Journalism," *Middle Eastern Studies* 28 (1992): 258–280.

16. Lynn Avery Hunt, *Politics, Culture, and Class in the French Revolution* (Berkeley: University of Californian Press, 1984).

17. Peter Burke, *Popular Culture in Early Modern Europe* (N.Y.: Harper Torchbooks, 1978).

18. *Kashkul* year 1, no. 10 (June 15, 1907).

19. His full name was Shaikh Ahmad Majd al-Islam Kirmani. According to Bamdad, he was born in 1872 and died in 1922. According to Browne, while he participated in the national movement by joining secret societies, starting the National Library, and editing newspapers, his character was under question as he was rumored to have taken bribes. Kasravi speaks of him only fleetingly and with contempt. Mahdi Bamdad, *Sharh-i Hal-i Rijal-i Iran*, v. 4 (Tehran: Kitabfurushi-i Zuvvar, 1347); E. G. Browne, *The Persian Revolution of 1905–1909* (London: Frank Cass, 1966 [1910]); and Ahmad Kasravi, *Tarikh-i Mashruta-yi Iran* (Tehran: Amir Kabir Press, 1370).

20. Raymond Williams, *The Sociology of Culture* (N.Y.: Schocken Books, 1981), p. 95.

21. Indeed, Vincent Rafael, in his study of nationalism in the Filipino context, argues that one of the central issues of nationalism revolves around "the problem of representation: who has the right to speak for whom and under what circumstances?" Vincent Rafael, "Nationalism, Imagery, and the Filipino Intelligentsia in the Nineteenth Century," *Critical Inquiry* (Spring 1990), p. 592.

22. The classic study of this subject appears in a monograph by Timothy Mitchell. See Mitchell, "Egypt at the Exhibition," in *Colonising Egypt* (Berkeley: University of California Press, 1991): 1–33.

23. *Kashkul* year 1, no. 9 (June 4, 1907), p. 3.

24. *Kashkul* year 1, no. 16 (August 10, 1907), p. 2.

25. For a seminal discussion of cultural hybridity in the context of colonial India, see Homi Bhabha, "Signs Taken for Wonders: Questions of Ambivalence and Authority Under a Tree Outside Delhi, May 1817," in *The Location of Culture* (London: Routledge, 1994): 102–122.

26. *Kashkul* year 1, no. 9 (June 8, 1907), p. 4.

27. *Kashkul* year 1, no. 20 (September 28, 1907), p. 2.

28. *Kashkul* year 1, no. 20 (September 28, 1907), p. 1.

29. Ibid.

30. *Kashkul* year 1, no. 1 (March 10, 1907), p. 4.

31. *Kashkul* year 1, no. 26 (November 23, 1907), p. 2.

32. I think a point that Gyanendra Pandey makes in the context of the historiography of nationalism in India is useful for us to bear in mind in the Iranian context as well. He wrote, ". . . the temptations of totalizing discourses are great. The yearning for the 'complete' statement, which leaves out nothing of importance is still with us. That urge will remain an important and necessary part of the historiographical endeavor. At the same time, however, it would be well to acknowledge the provisionality of the statements we make, their own historicity and location in a specific political context, and consequently their privileging of particular forms of knowledge, particular relationships and forces to the exclusion of others." Gyanendra Pandey, "In Defense of the Fragment: Writing About Hindu-Muslim Riots in India Today," *Representations* no. 37 (Winter 1992), p. 50.

33. Robert Darnton, *The Kiss of Lamourette* (N.Y.: W. W. Norton and Co., 1990), p. 107.

34. E. G. Browne, *A Literary History of Persia*, v. 4 (Cambridge: Cambridge University Press, 1959), p. 458.

35. Miles Taylor, "John Bull and the Iconography of Public Opinion in England c. 1712–1929," in *Past and Present* (1992): 93–128.

Bibliography

Afary, Janet. *The Iranian Constitutional Revolution, 1906–1911* (N.Y.: Columbia University Press, 1996).

Afshari, M. Reza. "The Historians of the Constitutional Movement and the Making of the Iranian Populist Tradition, "*International Journal of Middle East Studies* 25 (1993): 477–494.

Ayalon, Ami. "*Sihafa*: The Arab Experiment in Journalism," *Middle Eastern Studies* 28 (1992): 258–280.

de Baecque, Antoine. "The Allegorical Image of France, 1750–1800: A Political Crisis of Representation," *Representations* 47 (1994): 111–143.

Balaghi, Shiva. "The Iconography of Power: The Political Cartoons of *Kashkul* and the Anglo-Russian Convention of 1907," forthcoming.

———"The Iranian as Spectator and Spectacle: Theater and Nationalism in Nineteenth Century Iran," in *Social Constructions of Nationalism in the Middle East*, ed. F. Müge Göçek, forthcoming.

———"The Shift from the Manuscript to the Printed Book in Qajar Iran," working paper.

Bamdad, Mahdi. *Sharh-i Hal-i Rijal-i Iran*, v. 4 (Tehran: Kitabfurushi-i Zuvvar, 1347).

Bayat, Mangol. *Iran's First Revolution* (N.Y.: Oxford University Press, 1991).

Bhabha, Homi, "Signs Taken for Wonders: Questions of Ambivalence and Authority Under a Tree Outside Delhi, May 1817," in *The Location of Culture* (London: Routledge, 1994): 102–122.

Browne, E. G. *A Literary History of Persia*, v. 4 (Cambridge: Cambridge University Press, 1959), p. 458.

———"The Persian Press and Persian Journalism," text of lecture delivered to the Persia Society, May 23, 1913.

———*The Persian Revolution of 1905–1909* (London: Frank Cass, 1966 [1910]).

———*The Press and Poetry of Modern Persia* (Los Angeles: Kalimat Press, 1983 [1914]).

Brummett, Palmira. "Dogs, Women, Cholera, and Other Menaces in the Streets: Cartoon Satire in the Ottoman Revolutionary Press, 1908–11," *International Journal of Middle East Studies* 27 (1995): 433–460.

Burke, Peter. *Popular Culture in Early Modern Europe* (N.Y.: Harper Torchbooks, 1978).

Chartier, Roger. *The Cultural Origins of the French Revolution* (Durham: Duke University Press, 1991).

Geertz, Clifford. "Art as a Cultural System," in *Local Knowledge* (N.Y.: Basic Books, 1983): 94–120.

Hourani, Albert. *Arabic Thought in the Liberal Age, 1798–1939* (Cambridge: Cambridge University Press, 1983).

Hunt, Lynn. *Politics, Culture, and Class in the French Revolution* (Berkeley: University of California Press, 1984).

Kashkul.

Kasravi, Ahmad. *Tarikh-i Mashruta-yi Iran* (Tehran: Amir Kabir Press, 1370).

Keddie, Nikki. "The Assassination of Amin As-Sultan (Atabak-i A'zam) 31 August 1907," in *Iran and Islam: in Memory of Vladimir Minorsky*, ed. C.

E. Bosworth (Edinburgh: University of Edinburgh Press, 1971): 315–30.

Keddie, Nikki and Mehrdad Amanat, "Iran Under the Later Qajars, 1848–1922," *Cambridge History of Iran*, v. 7 (Cambridge: Cambridge University Press, 1991): 174–212.

Lewis, Bernard. *The Emergence of Modern Turkey* (Oxford: Oxford University Press, 1968).

Lockman, Zachary. "Imagining the Working Class: Culture, Nationalism, and Class Formation in Egypt, 1899–1914," *Poetics Today* 15 (1994): 157–190.

Mitchell, Timothy. *Colonising Egypt* (Berkeley: University of California Press, 1991).

Pandey, Gyanendra. "In Defense of the Fragment: Writing About Hindu-Muslim Riots in India Today," *Representations* 37 (1992): 27–55.

Rabino, H. L. *Surat-i Jarayid-i Iran va Jarayid-i ke dar Kharij-i Iran be Zaban-i Farsi Tab' Shudah Ast* (Rasht, 1329).

Rafael, Vincent. "Nationalism, Imagery, and the Filipino Intelligentsia in the Nineteenth Century," *Critical Inquiry* (1990): 591–611.

Sadr-Hashemi, Mohammad. *Tarikh-i Jarayid va Majallat-i Iran* (Isfahan, 1327), v. 4, pp. 135–137.

Sohrabi, Nader. "Historicizing Revolutions: Constitutional Revolutions in the Ottoman Empire, Iran, and Russia, 1905–1908," *American Journal of Sociology* 100 (1995): 1383–1447.

Taylor, Miles. "John Bull and the Iconography of Public Opinion in England c. 1712–1929," *Past and Present* (1992): 93–128.

Williams, Raymond. *The Sociology of Culture* (N.Y.: Schocken Books, 1981).

Wood, Marcus. *Radical Satire and Print Culture, 1790–1822* (Oxford: Clarendon Press, 1994).

From Cultural Schizophrenia to Modernist Binarism: Cartoons and Identities in Turkey (1930–1975)

AYHAN AKMAN

Introduction

This chapter explores the transformation of cartoons in Turkey from 1930 to 1975. Through the analysis of cartoons, it aims to understand the transformation of Turkish society, especially with respect to social and political identities. The first part with the period from 1930 to 1950, which is characterized by cultural schizophrenia. Cultural schizophrenia is the experience of split consciousness in which the local everyday life and an idealized western world are both embodied in the same habitus. The second period extends from 1950 to 1975 and is structured around binary oppositions, which are the hallmarks of a Modernist conception. The modernist understanding imposes its matrix of binary identities on the social and political practices of social actors.

In order to present an analysis of the changing identity structures in Turkey, this chapter will focus on the following aspects of cartoons:

1. Styles and techniques of cartooning (the technical and artistic conventions of drawing cartoons)

2. Representation of characters in cartoons (the "cast")

3. The modes of representation of social and historical spaces in cartoons (i.e. the specificity of non-discursive contextualization)

4. Prevalent themes and issues in cartoons

5. The "habitus" of the professional cartoonists (magazines, newspapers, competitions, circulation figures, associational life, etc.)

6. The self-perception of cartoonists (the way they discursively articulate their activity and their role)

Notwithstanding the technical, practical, and political differences separating these two periods (1930–50 and 1950–75), this chapter will try to show a surprising continuity between them on a more fundamental level. That continuity stems from the need to respond to the problem of Modernity. For the purposes of this chapter, we will understand by Modernity the creation of a modern(izing) world order ongoing since the middle of 16th century (Wallerstein, 1976; Braudel, 1992). In other words, the underlying problematique that creates the continuity between these two periods is the way in which the social consciousness of this "non-Western" society has been inflicted with the problematic presence of Modernity.[1]

This chapter's focus will be on two distinct patterns of responses to the problem of Modernity observed in the cartoons of the 1930–50 and 1950–75 periods. The two response configurations differ by the way they structure identity formations. These identity formations not only make an imprint on the political arena, which comprises official-institutional apparatuses, but to a large extent also shape the lived experience of everyday life. The different response configurations constitute the various strands of Modernism as a quasi-immanent, localized socio-political movement.

PART I
Two Worlds in Cartoons: Cultiral Schizophrenia (1930–1950)

The Social and Political Context of 1930

The year 1930 is a significant turning point both for the genealogy of cartoons and for the political superstructure in Turkey. The events clustering around 1930 justify its use as the departure point for our inquiry.

The years following the founding of the Republic in 1923 were marked by a series of modernist cultural and political reforms. This modernist drive was led by Atatürk and his cadre in the Republican People's Party (RPP). With the collapse of the Ottoman empire, this group, known as Kemalists, gained control of the new Republic. They were pro-nationalist reformists. Their rank consisted of military officials, bureaucrats, journalists and "intellectuals" in general. Despite their desire to differentiate themselves from the Ottoman legacy, Kemalists showed a significant continuation with the Ottoman reformist tradition. They were "heir[s] to the reformist legacy, with reformism widely understood as the successful adoption of Western forms." (Keyder, 1987: 141)

This reformist legacy manifested itself in the pursuit of "advanced civilization" by implementing reforms that would enable the county to "catch up with the West". Like their predecessors in the Ottoman Empire, Kemalists designed a whole series of cultural and political reforms in order to achieve parity in the interstate system. Raising the country to "the level of contemporary civilizations" was regarded as a fundamental but necessary step to achieve that goal. Unlike the Ottoman reformers, however, Kemalists' push for modernization was realized within the framework of a nation-state. Therefore, "modernization through Westernization became the Republic's supreme goal, and nationalism and secularism were used to implement it." (Karpat, 1959: 444) For Kemalists reformism, elitism, positivism, and statism went hand in hand.

The Kemalist reforms presented a project of modernity that aimed at building a new society based on principles of scientific rationality. The content of the cultural project articulated through these reforms was imported from the "advanced civilization" of the West with explicit acknowledgement. This "advanced civilization" was valorized for embodying the universal principles of science and rationality on the one hand and universal standards of humanity on the other.

The West became the criterion according to which all customs, norms and institutions were judged.[2] This resulted in the rejection and denunciation of many forms of the "local" culture. Reforms initiated by the Kemalist regime targeted everything from political institutions to units of measurement, from civic law to dress codes. The single party era (1930–1946), during which the Republican People's Party ruled uncontested, is the period during which Kemalism became the official state ideology.

1930 marks an important turning point regarding the nature of the political regime as well. With the disastrous ending of the second experiment with multi-party politics, the RPP consolidated itself as the ruling party. The Freedom Party was founded as a quasi-loyal oppositional party in 1930. Yet, after a short period of time, it showed signs of becoming a popular movement which could actually challenge the ruling RPP. The Freedom Party was declared closed the same year by its founders, who were concerned that the party was "getting out of hand." This declaration caused an angry reaction, and acts of violence were suppressed by the army. The RPP remained in power until 1950 without further challenges.

The consolidation of the new Republican regime under the leadership of the RPP was also facilitated by the onset of the World Depression in 1930. The Depression, as anywhere else in the world, resulted in a state-directed and state-controlled economy. This was harmonious with the RPP's desire to "modernize" the country while retaining the control of the political arena.[3] In brief, 1930 was a significant turning point for Turkish society in political, economic, and cultural terms. It fundamentally transformed the social, political, and economic matrix within which cartoonists worked.

A Period of Novelty and Innovation: Alphabet Reform and the Institution of "Civic Cartoons"

The many novelties and innovations observed in Turkish cartooning during this period hint at the thriving nature of cartooning despite economic depression, the Second World War, and the authoritarian single party regime.[4] During this period:

* Cartoons became a common feature in newspapers.[5]
* The first caricature contest was organized (Alsaç, 1994: 29).[6]
* The first cartoon exhibition was opened.[7]
* The first Turkish cartoon strip "Amcabey" was created.[8]
* The first attempt at cartoon animation was made.[9]
* For the first time a woman became a professional cartoonist.[10]
* It became common for cartoonists to publish their work in albums.[11]

Figure 1: One of Ramiz's cartoons (*Akbaba*, 1935)
—Where are you rushing?
—To congratulate a friend.
—How come? It's been a week since the holiday.
—Oh, no; he got three liras from the lottery, that's why.

Akbaba was the single most important cartoon magazine of this peri-od.[12]

Turkish media experienced a "culture shock" after the alphabet reform of 1928. By law, all publications were forced to begin using the Latin alphabet in a relatively short period of time. The result was disas-trous for print media, especially for newspapers and magazines. Even with government compensation, most newspapers had to shut down because of an all-time low circulation level. It was at this point that news-papers began turning toward graphic material in general, and cartoons in particular, to keep their readership from shrinking even further. The reac-tion of the readers to the introduction of daily cartoons and comic strips was very enthusiastic. At a time when the whole populace was struggling to become literate in the Latin alphabet, cartoons worked remarkably well at relieving the pressure of the new alphabet. When it became apparent that the newspaper *Akşam*'s contract with Cemal Nadir for daily cartoons was a success, it did not take long for the other newspapers to emulate this approach.

In significant part because of the appearance of cartoons in all major newspapers, cartooning, like journalism, became an accepted profession from 1930 onward. The professionalization of cartooning was a novel phenomenon. The cartoonists of the previous periods were usually not involved in cartooning as a full time professional activity but rather as an occasional or supplementary undertaking that they performed as "intel-lectuals-at-large." They were usually involved in other literary endeavors and frequently held positions in the state bureaucracy as well.

By contrast, the generation of cartoonist exemplified by Cemal Nadir (1902–1947) and Ramiz Gökçe (1900–1953) represents the dedicated, full-time, professional cartoonist for whom cartooning is the primary means of subsistence. It is this generation which began the process of cre-ating a distinct professional status for cartoonists.[13]

Cemal Nadir is widely acknowledged to be the single most important and influential cartoonist of this period (Yücebaş, 1950; Öngören, 1983; Özer, 1994; Alsaç, 1994). He was a prolific cartoonist who held the honor of being the creator of the first cartoon strip in Turkey.[14] Cemal Nadir is credited for inventing civic cartoons [*içtimai karikatür*] in Turkey. In Faruk Fenik's words:

At the time, there used to be two kinds of cartoons: cartoons centered around women, and political cartoons. The [genre of] "Women's cartoons" was already crowded. Thus, he [Cemal Nadir] chose to do political cartoons. Through his cartoons he was constantly criticizing the government. Thus, he increasingly

Figure 2: Local elements in Nadir's cartoons (Balcıoğlu, 1976: 191)
At the park's entrance:
Woman—If you could let us through,
we want to get into the park to get some fresh air!

became identified as the man with a cynical outlook. He found himself in a cul-de-sac. At this particular juncture, he discovered something important: the genre of civic cartoons. Instead of the government, he began targeting the community itself by satirizing its habits and customs. (Yücebaş, 1950: 123)

Civic cartoons became a form of communication regarding the experience of daily life in a big city. As Cemal Nadir himself remarks, "Caricature is no longer a fantasy or luxury; it has become a medium with which we can communicate each other our problems and our imperfections." (Yücebaş, 1950: 26) The focus on daily life and the thematization of the daily practices of the fellow residents of Istanbul distinguished Nadir's work from others by its civic character. His cartoons were the outgrowth of his experiences of the society in which he was embedded. He drew the stories of the social milieux that he inhabited. He satirized the customs, habits, and beliefs of the social world around him. His strong sense of social locatedness (of identifying with a particular location in a particular historical period) gave his work exceptional vitality and social relevance. The social locatedness of his cartoons has been acknowledged by many, including the legendary journalist Burhan Felek, who argued that "every day Cemal Nadir reports a different aspect of Istanbul." (Yücebaş, 1950: 27)

Cemal Nadir's cartoons took place in the shared spaces of everyday life in Istanbul. Şevket Rado's comment makes the same point: "I think Cemal Nadir's new cartoon album is the most perfect and most refined work that communicates, with its peculiar characters, happenstances and arrangements, about the era we live in, and analyses this world in all of its logical and illogical aspects, with all of its fearsome and cheerful features." (Yücebaş, 1950: 29)

Figure 3:
Cemal Nadir's Amcabey
(Yücebaş, 1950: 114).

Nadir's pragmatism and individualist attitude were the main reasons he refrained from committing himself and his work to any specific political agenda, ideology, or movement. Even though he was very much interested in social issues (thus pioneering "civic cartoons"), he refused to assume the role of a "vanguard". His interest in local and social phenomena stemmed not from an ideological preoccupation with social control and social reform, but from a practical, pragmatic interest in the concrete social conditions of his own existence. In this respect, his approach is strikingly similar to the understanding that began dominating cartoons in 1980s.

Two Worlds in Cartoon Form

The cartoons of this period manifest an intense case of cultural schizophrenia: The social world in these cartoons consists of two distinct and sometimes conflicting realms of cultural identity. The phenomenon of "identity split" in societies experiencing forced modernization and diachronic social change has been a common characteristic of the "third world countries" in their quest to survive in the modern world system (Shayegan, 1991).

The cartoons during 1930–1950 exhibit and embody two separate worlds. The cast of characters, drawing styles, and social spaces of these cartoons are almost entirely distinct. The two worlds correspond to:

1. The local and daily world of civil servants (*memur*) and small shopkeepers (*esnaf*) (see figures 1–4, 6–8 and 11), and

2. The idealized western world of balls, gowns, piano lessons, furs, beach parties, and ski resorts (see figures 5, 9, 10 and 12).

The style of drawing employed in depicting the idealized/Western world was that of illustration. The goal of attaining "realism" in representation resulted in a painting-like quality (see figures 5, 9, 10). This tendency was especially prevalent in cartoons depicting "high society" in general, and female figures in particular.

Perhaps the fact that this was an idealized or fantasy world may help to explain why the cartoonists opted for the realistic style. This was an idealized or "fantasized" world of what life is (or should be) in the "modern world." The cartoonists graphically construed this "modern world" not out of a direct or personal experience but, more likely, by reading glossy

Figure 4: An example of the "local world" in cartoons; dynamic and detailed depiction of daily life by Mazhar Nazım Telli (*Akbaba*, 1935). "At 8.00 in the morning; Life on the [Galata] bridge"

European magazines. Europe, representing the cultural model of "modern society" and "advanced civilization," was both a source and an inspiration for the cartoonists in creating this fantasy world where characters looked more "western" than westerners themselves. The use of realism in style suggests the cartoonists' desire to compensate for their lack of direct, daily, personal experience of the world they were representing.

The local, daily life cartoons, on the other hand, employed a novel style of representation. For the first time in Turkish cartoons, stylization became a technique of depiction. This involved omitting a lot of the details that illustration-type cartoons contained. It also involved the representation of the subjects by drawing their "typical" characteristics. The cartoons of this kind were considered to be "crowded" by the modernist cartoonists who emerged later, during 1950s. "Local" cartoons exhibited considerable detail and used secondary graphic elements that were not

Figure 5: Tuxedos and gowns; champagne; blue eyes and fair skin: "Modern personalities" [*Asri Şzahsiyetler*] by Ramiz (*Akbaba*, 1936).

directly related to the jokes' narrative structure. Yet, this inclusion of detail and secondary elements was not motivated by a realistic under-standing. Instead, these elements were selectively employed to create an "atmospheric effect" to complement the main narrative structure of the joke. They also helped to situate the joke socially, geographically, and historically.

Typical examples of this kind of stylization are good-luck beads hanging from the roofs of old Turkish houses, traditional heaters and mesmerized cats in front of them, minarets in the background, and flower pots in window frames. The stylization of the objects of daily life gave a peculiar local character to these cartoons. The modernist cartoonists of the following period (1950–1975) are characterized by their systematic avoidance of such forms of localism.

Figure 6: Depiction of the local world in rich graphic detail by Necmi Riza
(*Akbaba*, 1939).
—Oh, friend; our neighborhood has become just like [PM] Bayar's Cabinet;
there are no familiar faces!

Figure 7: Shopkeepers in the neighborhood (*Akbaba*, 1934)
Milkman—Oh, Ehmet; you hiked the prices for coal and wood again, huh?
Coal seller—Well, sonny; I don't get milk from tap water, you know!..

Figure 8: Detail: The civil servant and the small shopkeeper
(*Karikatür*, 1947)

Figure 9: Characters from the "western script" by Ramiz (*Akbaba*, 1935).
—Dear, why are you so sad?
—I lost my lover..
—Sorry to hear that; he was quite handsome. Whoever found him should be
very happy now!

Figure 10: The rich husband and the young wife (*Karikatür*, 1947):
—I dream of having a place in your heart.
—That could be arranged; of course if you are willing to pay the deposit for it!..

The local world of cartoons was created by cartoonists' direct and personal experience of their society. The daily experience of the peculiarities of their society was the "bread and butter" of these cartoonists' practice; this was where they found the thematic and humorous material that they worked into their cartoons. Thus, cartooning in this period provided the possibility of self-expression for the experience of the cartoonist in his daily "life-world." It was this routine expression of typical daily experience that was replaced with a universalist discourse in orienting the cartoonist to his society in the period after 1950.

The characters inhabiting the two worlds also differed significantly: the rosters of actors were from two different scripts. The characters from the "western" script usually looked as though they were taken out of the pages of some fashion magazine. Many of these cartoons evolved around the stereotypical couples of "elderly husband and young wife" (figure 10), or "young gentleman and beautiful girl." (figure 5) Cartoons centering on two (especially young) women were also very popular (figures 9 and 12). Curiously, it is impossible to find any cartoons in this genre that depict two (or more) men alone, without the company of a female. The figures in the Western world usually look as if they are posing for the reader.[15]

We have already mentioned that the "local cartoons" of this period became stylized expressions of the direct everyday life experiences of the cartoonists. A complementary aspect of this new form was that the cast of characters in the cartoons had a tendency to become stereotypical. The stylization of the graphic aspect was complemented by the stereotypification of the characters in the narrative of the cartoon. This new pattern found its best expression in the period's leading cartoonist, Cemal Nadir.

In addition to creating Amcabey (figure 3), Cemal Nadir also developed a whole series of popular characters [*tipler*].[16] The common denominator of all these characters is that they are stereotyped representations of the "local" world. Stereotypification was a novel technique, and Nadir was not alone in using it. Ramiz Gokce also used it successfully in creating his "Comez" and "Tombul Teyze ile Siska Dayi" characters. The commonly stereotyped characters of this period include civil servants, small shopkeepers, retirees, housewives, merchants, pawnbrokers, street vendors, and peasants (figures 2, 4, 7 and 8).

Another interesting, minute and yet pervasive, difference between the

Figure 11: Public spaces and crowded trams in Ramiz's
depiction of the "local world" (*Karikatür*, 1947)
—Please go ahead, Sir!..
—Oh, no; I insist, you go in first!

"western" and "local" cartoons concerns the presence (or absence) of large groups of people in cartoons. The "western" cartoons are characterized by the visual absence of multitudes whereas crowded scenes are very common in the "local" cartoons (see figures 4 and 11). Perhaps this could be explained by the fact that the spaces of the local cartoons are varied, and include trolleys, ferries, streets, offices, etc., while the "western" cartoons are largely confined to more "private" spaces, especially apartments. But, even when the creator of the "westernist" cartoon used public spaces (like the street or the beach), he refrained from depicting large numbers of people: Except for the cartoons that depict ballrooms, almost none of the cartoons adhering to the "western" script contained more than three or four people. The "painting"-like style may be responsible for this avoidance of

Figure 12: A typical cartoon of the idealized/Western world. The style of drawing is illustration-like and the characters are situated in private spaces. (*Karikatür*, 1947)

crowds. By reducing the number of people present in cartoons, greater visual and narrative emphasis can be placed on two or three characters who are depicted in a style of great "realistic" detail. Perhaps another reason is the difficulty of imagining the western model in any other context except in well-demarcated and isolated private spaces. The "unbearable imperfection" of the concrete, daily public life of the city would have made the characters, fashions, and styles of the western script look too irrelevant.

War Cartoons: A "Retro" Genre

Cartoonists after 1930 were successful in supplementing political affairs as the predominant theme in cartoons with a whole array of other topics and concerns. With the introduction of "civic cartoons," the intensely political focus of the cartoons of the pre-1930 era tended to dissipate. In the words of one student of the period, "A populist understanding that thematized the contradictions of daily life become predominant. The political cartoons observed during the Second Constitutional Era (1908–1918) gave way to cartoons that were depoliticized due to political censorship." (Turgut, 1986: 14)

There were "political" cartoons during this era, but they were concerned mostly with the Second World War. Even though Turkey retained its neutrality throughout the war, it none the less felt war's effects in manifold ways. A national enthusiasm is to be found in many of the cartoons of this era. The Second World War inflamed the anti-imperialist sentiments that had taken root especially during the War of Independence (1919–1923). Furthermore, the nationalist development program implemented after independence created an understandable enthusiasm regarding what were perceived to be the achievements of the young Republic.[17]

Stylistically, a significant attribute of these war cartoons is that the figures in them were frequently overwritten with names that identified what or whom they represented (see figure 13). This was a technique borrowed from the cartoons of late 19th and early 20th century. The curious fact is that this technique has already become outdated in 1930s, and yet, in war-related cartoons, this rather redundant symbolic form of representation was employed. As Alsac notes, this period witnessed the develop-

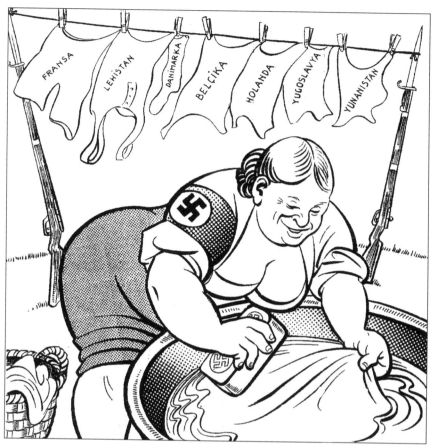

Figure 13: Clean-up on the Eastern Front:
—Either I am going to waste this bar of soap or really clean this sheet up!
(Behind her on the rope: France, Denmark, Belgium, Holland, Greece, etc.)
(*Karikatür*, 1941)

ment of a whole array of war-related symbols such as the Roman soldier (symbolizing war), the olive branch, or the white dove (symbolizing peace), the bear (symbolizing Russia), Uncle Sam (symbolizing the U.S.A.), or the fat cigar-smoking statesman in overcoat (symbolizing Britain). These symbols became the standard narrative tools in war-related cartoons (Alsaç, 1994: 27).[18]

Notwithstanding the "retro" character of war-related cartoons, on the whole, cartoons that looked like "illustrated jokes" became increasingly rare during this period. The verbal section was still indispensable and decisive in conveying the pun while a certain degree of simplification was also observed.[19] It was also during this period that cartoons without any verbal component made their historical debut.[20]

PART II:
Modernist Cartoons: Binary Identities (1950–1975)

Contextualizing 1950 as a Turning Point

1950 signals the beginning of a new era both for cartoons and for politics. In terms of cartoons, this is the beginning of a new understanding in cartoons and the assumption of a new role for the cartoonist. In 1950, the predominance of *Akbaba* magazine came to an end. Cartoon magazines multiplied and diversified in the 1950s. Parallel to this, a new generation of cartoonists emerged and dominated the scene. Variously called the "1946 generation," "1950 generation," or the "middle generation," this new breed of cartoonists espoused a new understanding in cartoons. Through the new magazines they began publishing, they developed "modernist cartoons" by redefining the artistic conventions as well as thematic concerns of cartoons. The transformation of the dominant style in cartoons and the changing understanding of cartooning were partly caused by the fact that the two great masters of the previous era died within a few years of each other. The loss of Cemal Nadir in 1947 and Ramiz Gokce in 1953 created a vacuum that facilitated the introduction and development of the modernist style. The eminent representatives of this new style were indeed students of the old masters and began their cartooning careers drawing like those masters. Nonetheless, they sought and formulated a new form of expression by revolutionizing the graphic form and thematic concerns of cartoons.

In addition, 1950 also represents an important date in terms of the wider social context. Authoritarian single-party rule came to an end in 1950 when the newly founded Democratic Party won the elections by a landslide. By 1950, Kemalists had lost their monopolistic claim to legitimacy and found themselves in the precarious position of having to respect the Democratic Party (DP) government elected by popular vote despite the fact that DP was giving up (or even reversing) some of the reformist policies of Kemalism. The tension progressively worsened as DP began using suppressive tactics against the opposition in the late 1950s. Finally, a military coup d'état, actively solicited and supported by the Turkish intelligentsia (including the cartoonists), ended the reign of the Democratic Party in 1960.

The transition to multi-party democracy in 1950 began re-defining various parameters of social life that had remained fixed throughout the era of the single party regime. Running on a platform of populism, pro-Islamic (or, folk-Islamic) sentiments and market economy, Democratic Party created a noticeable dynamism together with endless conflicts and controversies. This was the period immediately after the Second World War, a period of NATO membership, Marshall Plan assistance and the Green Revolution. The Democratic Party became the agent of this worldwide dynamism and change in Turkey. And it also experienced all the predicaments and contradictions that this dynamism entailed.

The 1960s witnessed the changing nature of the modernist cadres in Turkey. In addition to the Kemalist "old guard," there emerged a new generation of intellectuals and technocrats with leftist tendencies. For the first time in the Republic's history, a socialist party was able to gain representation in the National Assembly and voiced a loud protest. The transformation in the modernist cadres also coincided with the transition to an import substituting industrialization, on the one hand, and the emergence of a whole new understanding of the notion of "development," on the other.[21]

While the period from 1960 onward witnessed the rise of the left in Turkey in general, a parallel shift was also observed in the political convictions of cartoonists who now positioned themselves to the left of the political spectrum. They also began regarding their art as being inextricably intertwined with their political agenda. In brief, the period after 1950 is markedly different from the previous era both in terms of the general political and social context and in terms of cartoons.

New Dynamism in Cartoon Media

The decade of the 1950s witnessed a new dynamism and the prolif-eration of cartoon magazines. Breaking the virtual monopoly that *Akbaba* held over the cartoon media during 1930s and 1940s, numerous maga-zines emerged and shaped the cartooning field from 1946 onwards. They differed from *Akbaba* not only in terms of their cartooning style but also in terms of their desire to convey political messages. Magazines like *Markopaşa* (1946–1950) were at the forefront of this new era of political mobilization and activism. Espousing a staunchly anti-government posi-tion, *Markopaşa* created a nucleus of opposition by itself. Identifying with a broadly conceived "leftist" agenda, it was the first of its kind to introduce "class struggle" as a theme in cartoons and focus on social and political issues from a specifically leftist/progressivist perspective. Sup-porting a political agenda and a mission, *Markopaşa*'s cartoons were among the emerging modernist cartoons.

Tef is usually credited for being the richest and the most "cheerful" magazine of this period. The general agreement is that this was a maga-zine "deeply enmeshed in a cheerful celebration and enjoyment of the multi-party regime" and that "*Tef* was unwilling to take sides when party competition turned sour and consequently had to close down." (Öngören, 1983; 1439)

1960–75 presents a puzzling period for modernist cartoons. Despite their spectacular emergence and subsequent domination of the cartooning field, modernist cartoonists were not successful in publishing magazines after 1960. This was a rather disquieting state of affairs for the modernist cartoonists in an era during which their success in the international arena was building up and their political agenda was implemented after the 1960 coup d'état which they overwhelmingly supported.

The stagnation in magazine publishing contributed to the diversifica-tion of the cartoonists' interests. During the 1960s, they became interest-ed in animated cartoons, advertising, theater, pantomime, cinema, and even in three dimensional "sculpted-cartoons." Another consequence of the stagnation in the publishing scene was a deepened interest in interna-tional competitions and events. These events provided both sources of financial benefit and alternative sources of prestige.

Figure 14: The cartoon that brought Semih Balcıoğlu the Bordighera Golden
Palm Award (Italy) in 1973 (Özer, 1994: 119).

International participation before the 1950 generation was sporadic and accidental at best. With the advent of modernist cartoons, participation in international contests gained immense importance for the modernist cartoonists who were intent on proving the universal validity and significance of their work (figure 14). Winning international awards and trophies became a distinguishing mark of those cartoonists who had achieved "transnational" stature. The 1950s and 1960s constituted the "golden era" for modernist cartoonists. The quality and frequency of international awards and honors received by Turkish modernist cartoonists during this period was exceptional.

Cartoons with a Mission: Oppositional Cartoons

The 1950 generation introduced cartoons that were politically conceived and politically motivated. Their understanding of politics involved issues such as the unjust social order, class struggle, critique of the state, the functioning of democratic institutions, and the possibility of social and political revolution. The political regime, the economic order, the governing parties and elites were the main targets of the 1950 generation. The themes of the previous era regarding the everyday problems of urban life were replaced by these politically more ambitious themes. Ali Ulvi, one of the leading modernist cartoonists, formulates this shift of interest in the following manner:

> Caricature examines the relationship of man to man, man to nature, and man to society from a critical perspective. Paintings do not possess this quality. For caricature, however, this [criticism] is its raison d'être . . . Before our generation, caricature in Turkey was more individualist. It began becoming socially oriented—and I proudly refer to this—with our generation. That is the 1950 generation. Previously the subject of caricature was individual criticisms, bride/mother-in-law relations, or urban problems. Street vendors, rising costs of living, etc. Social themes entered caricature with the 1950 generation and prepared the reader for social criticism. That is, the reader also began expecting social criticism. What makes caricature "social" is its class orientation, and this began after 1950. (Ersoy, 1986: 67–68)

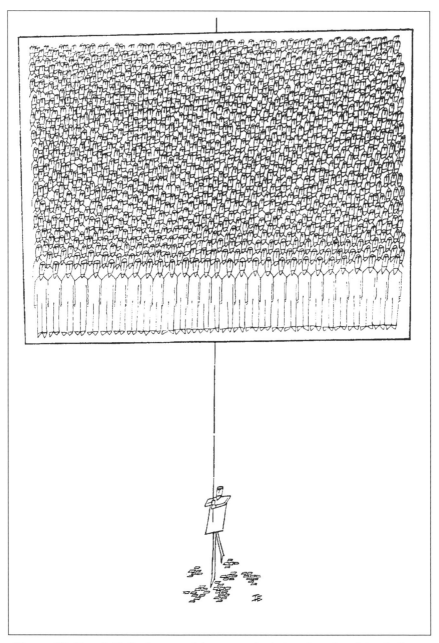

Figure 15: Ferruh Doğan's powerful cartoon depicting the role of the Artist as the vanguard of society (Balcıoğlu, 1976: 115).

The 1950 generation regarded politicization of cartoons not only as inevitable but also as desirable. In their view, cartoonists, as intellectuals, had a duty and responsibility to enlighten and educate the people. "Today's cartoonist has to wage the struggle in order to effect the changes that would transform our world." Selçuk, 1989; 97) They conceived their vanguard roles (figure 15), and justified them, by recourse to the universality of Reason and Science (to which, as intellectuals, they claimed to have privileged access). This understanding of the cartoonist as the vanguard with a moral and political mission is effectively voiced by Turhan Selçuk:

> The Artist is a vanguard of his society. It is natural for him to be revolutionary, progressivist, and against conservatism. In this respect, it is also natural for him to be against fascism, an outdated system of oppression. In essence, the contemporary cartoonist has to be fundamentally opposed to capitalism. (Selçuk, 1991: 26)

Their oppositional stance towards the "established order" coupled with a vanguard consciousness provided a new politicization of cartoons, significantly different from the earlier period. As Turgut (1986: 25) notes, "the essence of humor was conceived to be 'oppositional' in this era." Or, in cartoonist Tan Oral's words, "Oppressive and conservative governments constitute the primary area of interest for cartooning. The perpetual struggle [between oppressive government and cartoonist] continues until one of the parties is destroyed." (interview with Turgut, 1986: 37) Therefore, the new cartoonists viewed themselves as locked in a historical struggle against the established system of domination. This system of domination, in turn, referred either to the political regime or to the economic order; either to the state or to the bourgeoisie. Forming a political opposition became the main issue for the cartoonists of this era.[22] Thus, the cartoons were given the task of exposing and criticizing social injustices (see figures 16 and 17). The cartoons of this era were called "thought cartoons" (*düşünce karikatürleri*), indicating an urge for "consciousness-raising."

Modernist cartoons revolutionized cartooning in two interrelated senses. First, the graphic form of these cartoons was unprecedented; it

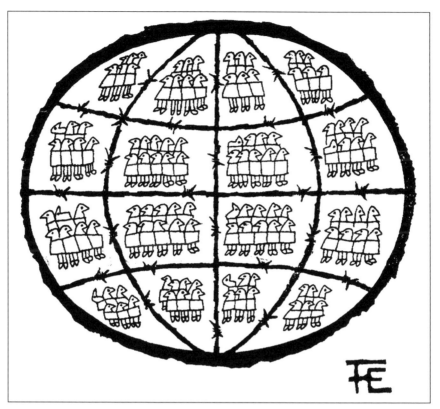

Figure 16: World as a prison (Doğan, 1969: cover).

broke with all the conventions of cartooning that previously existed. It
brought a fresh perspective to the possibilities that the practice of cartooning offered. It fundamentally altered the way cartoons were drawn, as
well as redefining their raison d'être. The established technique of cartooning that required a particular utilization of lines, shading, toning, and
dotting was overthrown. Use of words in cartoons began to be avoided.
In short, the graphic form of cartoons experienced a full-scale transformation.

The modernist understanding also revolutionized cartooning in the
sense that it closely allied itself with a leftist/modernist ideology. The
transformation in the graphic form of cartoons was accompanied by a parallel transformation of the thematic concerns of cartoons. As we have

Figure 17: A typical modernist cartoon by Meray Ulgen with leftist overtones (Balcıoğlu, 1976: 314).

already seen, issues like class domination, capitalism, and revolution became the prevalent topics of cartoons. Therefore, modernist cartoonists were revolutionary both in their graphic practice, which drastically transformed the conventions and techniques of the previous era, and in their espousal of a modernist/leftist ideology.

The Longing for the "Universal": Valorization of an Abrasive "Universality"

One of the modernist cartoonists' main ambitions was to create truly universal works of Art. The essence of Art (including the art of cartooning) was defined as the ability to transcend the boundaries of time and space. The distinguishing property of a true work of Art was its ability to speak the universal language of Humanity. Therefore, artificial barriers like language, tradition, and nationality were thought to interfere with the timeless appeal that a work of Art has to offer. In the words of one of these cartoonists: "History unfolds according to scientific laws. The cartoonist who is able to get the unchanging essence of the ever-changing everyday events will be able to produce works that will withstand the passage of time" (Selçuk, 1991: 26). Hence, the desire for universality entailed a desire for permanence and posteriority. In their typical Enlightenment view of the world and their work, modernist cartoonists aspired to rise to the level of Da Vinci, Michelangelo, or Beethoven in their work. Modernist cartoonists did not want to do merely local or daily cartoons. They wanted to produce works with universal value. Universality was the key to going beyond the merely temporal or ephemeral; to reaching a level that would be valid across cultures and time.

Figure 18: Tan Oral's cartoon thematizing the allegory of Enlightenment (Balcıoğlu, 1976: 238).

In their quest for the Universal, modernist cartoonists adopted a view of universality that was diametrically *opposed* to locality or particularism. In the modernist understanding, the Universal was precisely what the local or particular was *not*. In the tradition of the Enlightenment, they embraced universality at the expense of the local and the particular. The purification of the work of Art meant removing all the concrete social and historical details and connections. The "Universal" was understood to be that which is common to all Humanity; a level of generality that is not "tainted" with particularity, localism and tradition. Thus, the aim of the cartoonist was to discard, as much as possible, all traces of the local and particular. This purging of the contextual referents was regarded as a precondition for cartoons to become truly permanent and universal.

In short, in their quest to attain the Universal, modernist cartoonists slide into rejecting the social locatedness of both themselves and their work. The universalist understanding with which they operated prevented them from effectively articulating with the particular social-historical context in which they produced their work. Trapped by the binary dichotomy in which Universality was valorized as an *absolute* over and

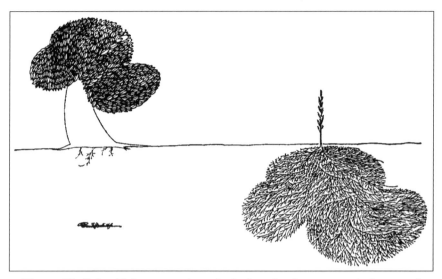

Figure 19: Balcıoğlu's cartoon is typical of modernist cartoons in its use of abstract graphic vocabulary to achieve universality (Balcıoğlu, 1971: 16–17).

against the merely local or particular, they were barred from searching for possible forms of hybridity of the universal and local on the one hand, and from the possibility of formulating incisive and successfully inter-ventionist oppositional cartoons (by the virtue of working with, rather than rejecting, their particular socio-historical context) on the other.

In contrast to the earlier cartoonists who regarded cartooning as a craft, modernist cartoonists worked to develop cartooning as an Art Form. They argued that it was with the emergence of modernist cartoons that cartooning finally became a true Art. "The controversy on whether caricature is an art form or not ended when the verbal element in cartoons was discarded and cartoons [of the previous period] evolved into graphic humor." (Selçuk, 1992) The role of the artist, the place of humor in soci-ety, the function of cartoons, universality in cartoons, and the political nature of cartooning were some of the issues that began to be discussed publicly.[23] The desire to articulate a systematic and theoretical view sug-gests the transformation of cartooning from an artisanal craft to "High Art."

A significant transformation that took place in this period resulted in the elimination of humor from modernist cartoons. As the modernist car-toonists became more politically ambitious and didactic, the presence of humor became increasingly precarious. Humor began to be seen as a problematic diversion (an auxiliary element of cartoons, at best) incom-patible with the demands of a politically motivated art. The demise of humor in modernist cartoons was a process coextensive with the loss of their popular appeal. As cartoons became more ideological, preoccupied primarily with conveying messages, they also became unappealing for the wider social audience. Therefore, in 1970s modernist cartoons increas-ingly became marginalized in terms of their popular appeal.

Steinberg's Influence: Transplantation and Transfiguration of an Aesthetic Style

The emergence of modernist cartoons fundamentally transformed the practice of cartooning in Turkey. And yet, its emergence was influenced by a new style of cartooning that was being developed in the West. It was Saul Steinberg and the "New Yorker Style" that he helped develop in the 1940s that became immensely influential in Turkey during the 1950s and throughout 1960s.[24] Steinberg's style was characterized by simple, single-line drawings devoid of any verbality. Thematically, Steinberg produced highly abstract and intellectual cartoons. It is frequently argued that it was Steinberg's influence that led Turkish cartoonists to simplify and "purify" their drawings. This simplification involved getting rid of unnecessary details and eliminating verbal segments from their cartoons. Turhan Selçuk attests to the influence of Steinberg quite explicitly:

> In our times, the most influential cartoonists were Cemal Nadir and Ramiz. I was trying to avoid that influence . . . yet, I was not drawing in a very simple and unadorned way. I had not yet reached my current level of simplicity [*sadelik*]. During the 1950s, when I saw Steinberg's cartoons, I understood what I needed to do. He is considered the father of modern cartoons, and he indeed is. (Selçuk, 1983)

In addition to stylistic influences concerning depiction techniques, Turkish cartoons also begin to use new themes and symbols imported from the West.[25] Even though Steinberg's style was imported from the West, the particular way in which it was appropriated showed significant differences from its original context. The New Yorker style cartoons can be classified as "Salon Cartoons," basically satirizing the conventions of urban bourgeois lifestyle in a light manner. The cliches of the "psycho-analyst's couch" or "lover hiding in the closet" are perfect examples of this. The stone age and deserted island type of cliches are similar in nature. It is the non-political character and indeed the superficiality of these cartoons that was transfigured by modernist cartoonists in Turkey.

The appropriation of the New Yorker style by Turkish cartoonists was a very selective process. While the decontextualized and abstract style of Steinberg's cartoons was adopted, it was coupled with a univer-salistic social agenda and a class-based didactic and missionary attitude. The "Turkish blend" of modernist cartoons was motivated by political concerns to a remarkable extent (see figures 17, 20, 21 and 27). The apo-litical, light tone of the "salon cartoons" was superseded by a more ambi-tious attitude of conveying certain ideological messages through abstract and universalist artistic perfection. Ali Ulvi attests to this blending of rev-olutionary ideology with a formal and abstract style: "My generation has adapted the non-verbal humor of the artistic caricatures of the Western world to political and social issues and causes." (Ersoy, 1991: 33) Cartoons based on the deserted island type of thematic schema tended to disappear towards the middle of the 1960s. They were replaced by more political cartoons that were militant, programmatic and didactic.

From the mid-1960s onwards, modernist cartoons' loss of their audi-ence coincides with the emergence of a new and politically agitated young generation of modernist cartoonists. With the 1970 generation, the modernist cartoons became progressively more political, programmatic and agitated. This young and militant generation was inclined to use car-tooning as "weapon" in a broader social and political struggle. Their "left-ist" ideology persuaded these cartoonists to adopt an instrumentalist view of their practice in the service of class struggle.[26] It is through the institu-tional network Cartoonists' Association (founded in 1969) that modernist cartoons survived, however marginalized, in the 1970s and 1980s.

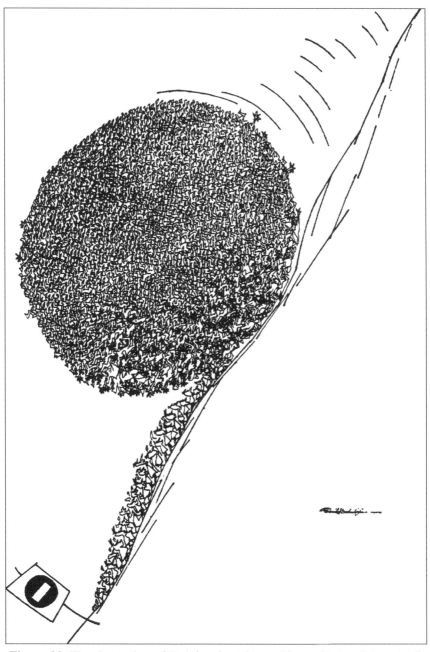

Figure 20: The abstraction of Steinberg's style combines with "social content" in this Balcıoğlu cartoon (Balcıoğlu, 1971: 35).

Figure 21: The idolization and downfall of "political leaders" was a popular theme for many modernist cartoonists including Turhan Selçuk (Selçuk, 1989: 92).

The Graphic Form of Modernist Cartoons

The period after 1950 is characterized by a transition to abstract and decontextual cartoons that exhibit minimalist graphic representation. The perspectival sketches of the previous era were superseded by a two-dimensional approach. Silhouettes without depth, shadow, or extension began to appear in the cast of cartoon characters. Simplification of the drawing [*çizgi*] became mandatory and details were permitted only to the extent that they enhanced the message of the cartoon (Selçuk, 1989: 97).

A certain abstract "hardness" in presentation became the hallmark of the modernist era. Backgrounds in cartoons disappeared. "In this period, Turkish cartoonists used the single-line [*tek çizgi*], volumeless [*hacımsız*] conception of cartooning." (Hünerli, 1993: 41) An abstract, homogeneous space emerged in which figures in cartoons were located. Techniques of shading, toning and coloring fell into disrepute alongside the repudiation of the perspectival approach. (Alsaç, 1994: 28)

The verbal component of cartoons was eventually completely elimi-

nated. The understanding that cartoons should be purely graphic
became dominant. Verbal sections
in cartoons came to be looked upon
with distaste and even contempt.
The following remark of Andre
Baur on Turhan Selçuk's cartoons is
a typical example:

> Words? . . . They distort the
> aesthetic balance of the
> work. If the message is
> clear, why erect an artificial
> language barrier? . . .
> humorous graphic represen-
> tation [çizgi] does not need
> extra explanations. This
> makes it all the more valu-
> able from an artistic point
> of view, and enables it to
> capture the universal lan-
> guage. (Baur, 1993)

In other words, verbality was
regarded as a "vice" cartoonists
resorted to when their creativity
with graphic elements failed.
Therefore, a perfect cartoon was the
one that was able to express its
"idea" purely through graphic representation. Verbal elements could, in
the most compelling cases, be used
as "crutches" to help convey the
"idea," but such help in effect meant
that the cartoon failed to conform to
the ideal. An additional and perhaps
equally crucial reason why verbality

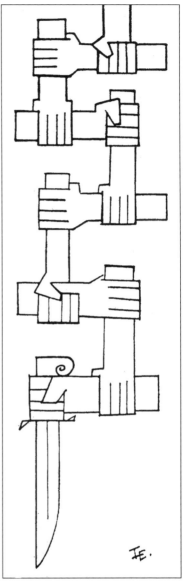

Figure 22: Ferruh Doğan created
some of modernist cartoons'
sharpest images by combining a
minimalist strategy of representation with piercing political
commentary (Doğan, 1969: 88).

was unwelcome in the modernist cartoons was that it was considered to hinder "universality." Since some translation would be needed for a cartoon outside of its original linguistic context, this was taken to mean a failure to convey the "idea" in a universal, graphic manner. The need for translation was seen as an imperfection in the art of cartooning. The prevailing idea was that true art should be perceivable purely and directly in its self-contained presence without requiring any translations or explanations. Consequently, verbality became a sign of banality and inferiority. The universalist understanding that decontextualized the cartoons and abstracted the figures in them, also eliminated verbality from cartoons.

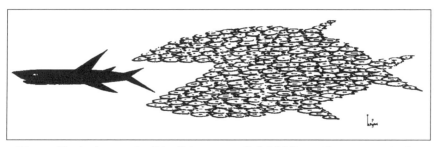

Figure 23: A play on the "big fish eats small fish" idiom. The message? The possible success of the political solidarity of the masses (Selçuk, 1989: 86).

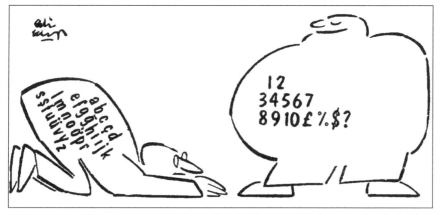

Figure 24: Characters as two dimensional silhouettes. Also note the lack of background and the homogeneity of the space in which figures are situated. By Ali Ulvi (Balcıoğlu, 1976: 156).

With the advance of the modernist understanding, the figures in cartoons began to lose their everyday familiarity. The daily life which had supplied the cast of characters in Cemal Nadir's era lost its relevance for this new generation of cartoonists who were interested in capturing the universal. Simultaneously, as the practices of daily life lost their hold on the social imagination of the cartoonists, the prescriptive logic of universalism filled in the gap. The decontextualization of the cartoons' spaces was in fact a recontextualization into a matrix of enlightenment rationalist universalism. There was, however, a price to be paid in this attempt to attain the universal: The loss of concreteness and richness of the local/daily life. The ambition for transcendence was construed in way that denied the local, the particular, and the present access to graphic representation. In a sense, this was a "utopian universalism" in which abstract human silhouettes stood for agency of social actors, and universal symbols stood for the substantiality of social life.

In earlier periods, perspectival illustration was the main instrument cartoonists used to situate their characters socially and historically by cushioning them in greatly elaborated backgrounds. Modernist cartooning identified itself and its social world with an "Idea-System" [*düşünce sistemi*]. Therefore, its social reality tended to be idealistic and prescriptive.

Binary Identities in Graphic Form

Modernism, in the context of identity formations in Turkey, provides a definite structuring principle: Binarism. The Modernist logic presents a specific matrix consisting of a finite set of possible identity categories. The self-contained economy of binary oppositions constitutes the logic of Modernist identities. Modernism also provides a self-enclosed space of historical development demarcated and organized according to the contrast offered by the binary categories of identity.[27]

Modernist cartoons use a series of binary oppositions to construct their social and political universe. The dualisms of civilized versus backward, West versus East, worker versus capitalist, poor versus rich, etc., permeate these cartoons in such a way that the cast of characters is always in a relationship of unresolvable conflict (see figures 24, 26 and 27).

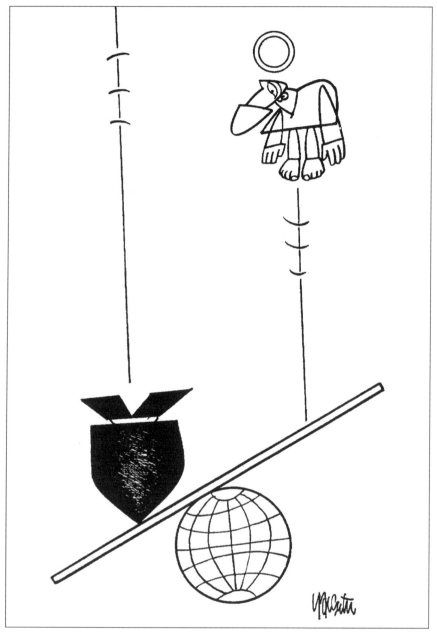

Figure 25: Didacticism goes hand in hand with the use of "universal" symbols in Yalcin Cetin's cartoon. Note how "space" becomes "surface," indicating decontextualization (Balcıoğlu, 1976: 99).

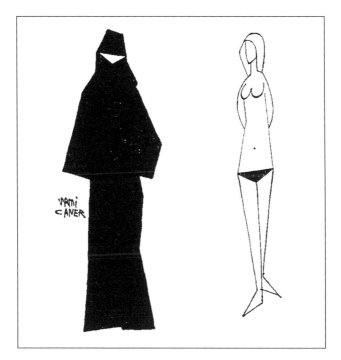

Figure 28: Sami Caner's depiction of two women
embodying opposite poles of the binary matrix of
identities: modern versus traditional, West versus East,
progressive versus backward, etc. (Balcıoğlu, 1976: 88)

In addition to being dualistic, modernist identities in cartoons also
have a symbolic character. In their abstraction, they always stand for
something other (and larger) than themselves. Modernist cartoons have
no individualized characters. The figures are always the prototypical representations of some larger group or social class. As such, the individual
figures (when they exist) have no individuality; they are interchangeable
units of a larger whole, members of a group or class (see figures 15, 16
and 28). The decontextual character of these cartoons also works to create the same effect; stripped of any reference to the concrete, present
social context, the abstract characters in these cartoons "drift" in homogeneous space.

Figure 27: Suha Bulut's cartoon manifests a version of modernist binarism based on class antagonism. A.S. in Turkish means "Inc." and AS means "food" (Balcıoğlu, 1976: 86).

While decontextualization allowed modernist cartoonists to utilize a symbolic vocabulary that aimed at capturing Universality, it also barred them from a possible (if critical) articulation with the concrete practices of everyday life. In their rejection of the given social order as illegitimate, they began to speak from a decontextualized and ahistorical subject position.

The avant-garde aspirations of these cartoonists already hints at such an acute disarticulation from present social reality. What makes modernist cartoons so striking, however, is the degree to which their human figures become generic and abstract. In a way, the decontextualizing move of modernist cartoonists transforms the rich and schizophrenic representation of characters of the 1930–50 period into abstract and generic figures that exist in two-dimensional space. Furthermore, these figures

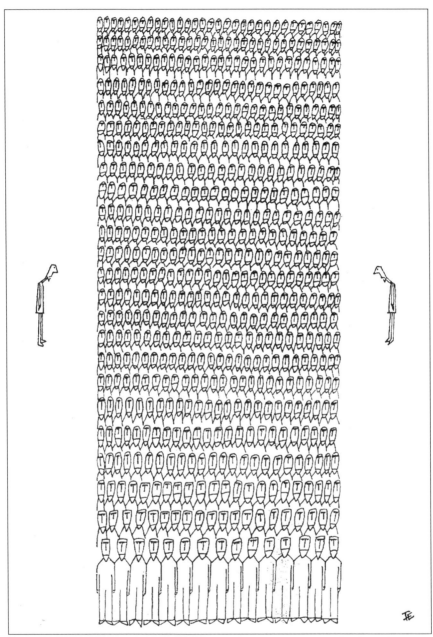

Figure 28: Interchangeability of characters and decontextualization of space are conspicuous features of Modernist cartoons like this one by Ferruh Doğan (Balcıoğlu, 1976: 114).

are always construed in a binary relationship whose interaction with each other is always structured around a central conflict.

* * * * * * * *

The presence of the problem of Modernity is recast in modernist cartoons in such a way that it eradicates the complex schizophrenic topography of the identity field of 1930s and establishes a tight matrix consisting of binary identity categories. The social and historical space within which these identities are situated is "flat" and homogeneous; its notion of historicity is unilinear and developmentalist.

The extrinsic and problematic coexistence of two different kinds of habitus that we observed in the "two worlds" of the 1930s is replaced by a modernist model that structures the identity field more directly and perhaps more successfully during the 1960s. The double "cast" of characters found in "two worlds" is reduced to a single cast. This is achieved, however, by radically abstracting the characters. This abstraction works on two levels: On one level, it entails a decontextualization of the social and historical space of those characters. On another level, it occasions the subsumption of these characters under a generic (class or group) identity category. Characters become interchangeable units of a larger whole: They belong to a generic identity category situated in a binary matrix whose telos is pre-determined by the way the matrix itself is structured.

Notes

1. The conventional view on Modernity regards it as a collection of norms and institutions as they have developed in the "West." According to this view, Modernity is the embodiment of a Western cultural model. The developmentalist view in its general outline embraces this view (see Almond and Powell, 1966; Huntington, 1968). An alternative view of Modernity conceptualizes it as an immanent process of self-directed social change (see Touraine, 1977; Göle, 1986).

2. The alphabet reform was a part of this general reform movement. In 1928, the alphabet was changed almost overnight from Arabic to Latin. This was another instance of the new Republic's desire to sever its links with the past, particularly its desire to dissociate itself from the Ottoman legacy. Through

the implementation of the reforms, the Republic was intent on engineering a new society for which the "West," being the archetype of "advanced civilization," served as a positive model. Alphabet reform was an important step in approximating that civilization.

3. The reform of the economy entailed the nationalization of foreign investments, a drive for industrialization, and the building up of a national infrastructure. These initial goals of the new regime eventually became its proudest achievements.

4. These innovations and novelties were propelled by the presence of a lively cartoon media. In 1938, for example, there were 7 cartoon magazines in publication (see Öngören, 1983: 1433). Furthermore, newspapers' daily featuring of cartoons and comic strips also led to a diversification of the cartoon media.

5. Cemal Nadir paved the way by drawing regularly in newspaper *Akşam* from 1928 onwards.

6. The first caricature contest was organized not by a cartoon magazine but by *Akşam*, a leading newspaper, in 1936.

7. It exhibited the works of Cemal Nadir in a "Halkevi" (a widespread chain of cultural centers founded by RPP).

8. Amcabey was created by Cemal Nadir in 1929 (see Figure 3).

9. Cemal Nadir attempted to create an animated film using his Amcabey character (Alsaç, 1986: 57).

10. Selma Emiroğlu, who was a student of Cemal Nadir, represents both the professionalization of cartooning and the new Republic's relative success in incorporating women into the public sphere with equal legal status.

11. This was the period during which cartoon albums were transformed from isolated instances to widely circulated public items. Cemal Nadir's "Amcabey'e Göre" (1932) was the first album published in this period. It was followed by Togo's album in 1937. Between 1937 and 1948, 34 caricature albums were published (Öngören, 1983: 1434). Cemal Nadir alone published 10 albums between 1932 and 1936. He published 7 more during 1940–1946.

12. Beginning publication in 1922, *Akbaba* earned the distinction of being the longest lasting humor magazine in Turkey. When it was finally forced to close down in 1977, it had a record-breaking 55 years behind it.

13. The other important cartoonists of the period include Orhan Ural, Necmi Riza, Kozma Togo, Riza Ayca and Ratip Tahir. The continuous production of these cartoonists was crucial in sustaining the vitality of the cartoon media. Yet, in terms of their understanding of cartoons and their style of

drawing, they were not as original and innovative as Nadir or Gökçe.

14. He was also the first cartoonist to become a regular contributor to a major newspaper. His cartoon exhibitions were the first individuated exhibitions of their kind and he was also the first to experiment with cartoon animation in Turkey.

15. One funny and yet pertinent way to distinguish the characters from the "western" cast and the "local" cast is to see if they have mustaches. Almost without exception, men in the "western" cast never have no mustaches, whereas almost every single male in the "local" cast (irrespective of social class or status) have one. The presence of the mustache is an indicator of the cartoonist's sense of social locatedness within the "present," characterized by his daily social life; it is the acknowledgement of his locatedness within the imperfect world of his concrete historical existence.

16. "Dalkavuk" [Mr. Brown Nose], "Akla Kara" [The White and the Black], "Yeni Zengin" [Nouveaux Riche], "Dedeyle Torun" [Grandpa and Grandson], and "Salomon" [Jewish Merchant] were among his well-known characters.

17. Viewed against such a background, it is not surprising to find cartoons attacking Russia, Germany, or Britain as potential threats, valorizing Turkish military strength, or emphasizing the assertions of self-sufficiency and self-reliance of the new Republic.

18. In addition to war related cartoons, the period also witnessed the emergence of other symbols related to cartooning as a medium of expression. Some of the new symbols borrowed from cartoons in the West included the popping hat symbol and stars circling the head of a dizzy person.

19. A subtle but revealing example of this trend for simplification is that the identity of the person speaking in the cartoon was no longer separately depicted in the verbal section below the graphic segment. Instead, the assumption that the graphic representation is enough to convey the identity of the voice speaking increasingly gained acceptance (Alsaç, 1986: 59).

20. Cemal Nadir was the pioneer in this new trend, as he was in many others. His "wordless" strips were the first of their kind in Turkey.

21. Ideas of planning and rational organization that large segments of the new leftist elites espoused reveal an underlying continuity with the Ottoman, and later Kemalist, reformist legacy which emphasized Science, Reason and Order over tradition and superstition. "The voluntarist revolutionaries [i.e. new leftists], more than anything else, are the inheritors of the positivism and centralism of the old modernizing elites." (Göle, 1986: 72)

22. So important was the idea of humor-as-opposition in the understanding of

the modernist cartoonists that they regarded periods of democracy and prosperity as being detrimental to having a lively cartooning scene. It was argued
that once the "enemy" or "problem" was overcome, there would not be much
need for opposition, and consequently not much need for cartooning
(Conversation with Tan Oral: 1994).

23. Of particular salience was the discussion centering around the question:
"should cartoons make people laugh or think". In other words, the issue of
the entertaining versus educating character of cartoons became a central one
during the ascendancy of the modernist understanding. The talk of "duties
and responsibilities" became a dominant discourse among the cartoonists.

24. In addition to Steinberg, a number of other cartoonists also made an impact
on the 1950 generation. A partial list of these cartoonists includes Chaval,
Bosc, Sempe, Moss, Flora, Topor, Sine, Gulbrasson, Andre Francois, and
Gurmelin.

25. Deserted island, lion-tender, eskimo, Indian snake dancer, Mickey Mouse,
stone age, Adam and Eve, doctor's office, psychoanalyst's couch, Statue of
Liberty, prison fugitives with striped uniforms, cowboys and Indians, the
lover hiding in the closet, all constituted the symbolic vocabulary of "Salon
cartoons" that were popular in the West during this period.

26. The 1970 generation sought to develop close ties with labor unions, cooper-
atives, and other mass organizations both as a matter of institutional back-
ing of their cartoons and as a matter of ideological allegiance. Yet, direct and
organic political engagement created tensions in the modernist understanding between the practice of their art form (with its own distinctive "logic,"
rules and conventions) and the political allegiances and motivations of its
practitioners.

27. The self-enclosed character of the Modernist system combines with the
binary codification of identities to produce the well-known narrative of
"development". This narrative views History as a process of traveling from
one pole of the binary equation to the other (e.g. from Traditional to
Modern). The space within which the telos of development unfolds is, thus,
necessarily contained within the matrix of binary identities.

References

Almond, Gabriel, and Bingham Powell, eds., 1966. *Comparative Politics: A Developmental Approach*. Boston: Little, Brown and Co.
Alsaç, Üstün, 1994. *Türkiye'de Karikatür, Çizgi Roman ve Çizgi Film*. İstanbul:

İletişim Yayınları.

Alsaç, Üstün, 1986. "Türk Karikatürü Üstüne Bir Döküm ve Eleştiri Denemesi." *Adam Sanat* no. 7, June, pp. 55–66.

Balcıoğlu, Semih, and Ferit Öngören, eds., 1976. *50 Yılın Türk Mizah ve Karikatürü*. İstanbul: İş Bankası Kültür Yayınları.

Balcıoğlu, Semih, 1971. *Yazısız Çizgiler*. İstanbul: Cem Yayınevi.

Baur, Andre, 1993. "Estetik bir Dehanın Evrensel Bakışı." *Cumhuriyet*, 7 February.

Braudel, Fernand, 1992. *Civilization and Capitalism, 15th–18th Century, Vol. III: The Perspective of the World*. Berkeley, CA: University of California Press.

Doğan, Ferruh, 1969. *Çizgili Dunya*. İstanbul: Ant Yayınları.

Ersoy, Ali Ulvi, 1991. "Zamanım Varsa Kafamla Cizerim." *Babıali Magazin* no. 25, 15 June/15 July, pp. 32–35.

Ersoy, Ali Ulvi, 1986. "Çizgi ile Düşünen Adam: Ali Ulvi (Turgut Çeviker ile Söylesi)." *Adam Sanat* no. 11, October, pp. 65–70.

Göle, Nilüfer, 1986. *Muhendisler ve İdeoloji: Öncü Devrimcilerden Yenilikçi Şeçkinlere*. İstanbul: İletişim Yayınları.

Hünerli, Selçuk, 1993. "Türkiye'de Gazete Karikatürünün Durumu ve Siyasi Karikatürün Söylemi." Master's thesis, Istanbul University.

Huntington, Samuel, 1968. *Political Order in Changing Societies*. New Haven: Yale University Press.

Keyder, Cağlar, 1987. *State and Class in Turkey: A Study in Capitalist Development*. London: Verso.

Karpat, H. Kemal, 1959. *Turkey's Politics: The Transition to a Multi-Party System*. Princeton: Princeton University Press.

Öngören, Ferit, 1983. "Türk Mizah ve Karikatürü." *Cumhuriyet Dönemi Türkiye Ansiklopedisi* vol. 5–6, İstanbul: İletisim Yayınları, pp. 1426–1455.

Öngören, Mahmut Tali, 1986. "Radio and Television in Turkey." In *The Transformation of Turkish Culture*, edited by Gürsel Renda and C. Max Kortepeter. Princeton: Kingston Press, pp. 179–196.

Özer, Atila, 1994. *İletişimin Çizgi Dili Karikatür*. Eskişehir: Anadolu Universitesi Yayınları.

Selçuk, Turhan, 1992. "Turhan Selçuk ve 50. Sanat Yılı Sergisi." *Milliyet* 12 January.

Selçuk, Turhan, 1991. "Keskin Çizgilerle Turhan Selçuk." *Babıali Magazin* no. 21, 15 February/15 March, pp. 24–27.

Selçuk, Turhan, 1989. *Grafik Mizahın Büyük Ustası: Turhan Selçuk*. İstanbul: Tuyap Yayınları.

Selçuk, Turhan, 1983. "Turhan Selçuk: Boş Zaman Diye Bir Şey Bilmiyorum." *Cumhuriyet* 16 April.

Shayegan, Daryush, 1991. *Yaralı Bilinç: Geleneksel Toplumlarda Kültürel*

Şizofreni. İstanbul: Metis Yayınları.

Steinberg, Saul, 1965. *The New World*. New York: Harper & Row.

Touraine, Alain, 1977. *The Self-Production of Society*. Chicago: University of Chicago Press.

Turgut, Erhan, 1986 "Türkiye'de Karikatür Santının Basındaki Yeri." Master's thesis, Istanbul University.

Wallerstein, Immanuel, 1976. *The Modern World System I: Capitalist Agriculture and the Origins of the European World Economy in the 16th Century*. New York: Academic Press.

Yücebaş, Hilmi, 1950. *Bütün Cepheleriyle: Cemal Nadir*. İstanbul.

"Gulf Laughter Break": Cartoons in Tunisia During the Gulf Conflict

MOHAMED-SALAH OMRI

The Persian Gulf crisis of 1990–91 was one of those moments when global tensions flared up and repressed hopes erupted to the surface seeking articulation. The impact of the conflict on the people and governments of the Maghreb was immediate and pervasive. The overwhelming popular protest and support for Iraq in the region is often attributed to domestic economic and political strife. Thus, people, in the words of David Seddon, "channeled much of their anger and dissatisfaction with their governments into support for Iraq" (Bresheeth, *Gulf and World Order*, 104).[1] The schism between the governments and their peoples in the region is indeed real and merits to be underscored. Yet it is only part of the story. Focus on the rift between the two does not account for the interplay between popular and official responses to the conflict, for instance. Neither does it address concerns that transcend the domestic issues brought to the surface by the crisis, such as the presence of a repressed anti-American sentiment, a lingering pan-Arab feeling, and, most importantly, a reading of the crisis as a historical opportunity to turn events around and correct endured injustices. The present essay gauges public opinion at the time of the conflict through cartoons published in Tunisian Arabic and French newspapers from the beginning of January until the end of March, 1991. It shows as well how the crisis affected the art of cartoon itself. In a country where the state usually kept a tight grip on the press and controlled public opinion, a better insight into public culture during the Gulf conflict will benefit from an examination of the official response to the crisis and why the Tunisian government reacted the way it did.

Official Responses

Tunisia's official position reflected the concerns of a new government, careful to preserve the country's regional alliances and close Western ties yet eager to distance itself from the regime it had recently removed and to consolidate its authority domestically.[2] This was perhaps why in foreign policy, the new government adopted an approach that combined caution, which had become the hallmark of Tunisia under Bourguiba, and a mild degree of assertiveness. Tunisia absented itself from the Arab Summit of August 10; it condemned the resolution of the U.N. Security Council to authorize the use of force to enforce sanctions against Iraq; and denounced the war itself in January 1991.[3] But throughout the crisis Tunisia maintained its commitment to a negotiated Arab solution. This policy was devised, in part, in coordination with Tunisia's immediate neighbors and in an effort to minimize the repercussions of the conflict on the Union of the Arab Maghreb (U.A.M.) comprised of Mauritania, Morocco, Algeria, Tunisia, and Libya. The five North African states did not see eye to eye at the beginning of the crisis. Mauritania expressed reservations against the resolution proposed at the Cairo Arab Summit of August 10, Algeria abstained, Libya rejected it, Morocco supported it and Tunisia absented itself.[4] Among the U.A.M. members, Morocco was certainly the most open in its support for the Gulf states despite the massive popular demonstrations for Iraq in the country, while Mauritania spearheaded the pro-Iraqi effort. Their positions, however, drew closer as the crisis escalated into war and as popular pressure throughout the Maghreb increased.[5] Due in part to continued coordination throughout the war, the U.A.M. would emerge from the crisis as the one Arab block that tried to preserve coherence and unity. Seddon notes that "despite differences, the Maghreb governments (particularly those of Morocco, Algeria and Tunisia) made a consistent effort to develop a coherent approach to a negotiated settlement whose key elements includ-ed: the withdrawal of Iraqi forces from Kuwait, the withdrawal of foreign forces from the Gulf and an 'Arab solution' to the crisis" (Bresheeth, *Gulf and World Order*, 106). Tunisia was instrumental in this respect.

The foreign policy of the new government was not, however, without domestic concerns, and had a considerable impact on events inside Tunisia. Popular response in the country was immediate, loud, and wide-spread. It took the shape of demonstrations, donations, and volunteering to join the Iraqis.[6] Such support pressured the government to align itself with the people and was in turn strengthened as the government came per-haps closer to popular sentiment than ever before. Zoubir writes: "Unlike what happened in the 1967 and 1973 Arab-Israeli wars, the position of the government and the opposition converged. President Zine El Abidine Ben Alī espoused the public sentiment—perhaps to control the Islamic funda-mentalists who could have exploited the situation to their own advantage as did the Algerian Islamists—and obtained unanimous support from the legal opposition parties" (Zoubir, 92). Two speeches by President Ben Alī, at the start and at the end of the war, illustrate the new government's position. In the first, delivered on 26 January, Ben Alī "approved of the strong feelings of the Tunisian people regarding 'the intolerable destruc-tion and devastation of Iraq' and the suffering of the Iraqi people and also their control and restraint in expressing their feelings of anger and out-rage" (Bresheeth, *Gulf and World Order*, 110). In the speech of 25 February, after reiterating his rejection of the coalition's "deliberate" destruction of Iraq, Ben Alī urged Tunisians to think of the future and "to unite in their commitment to resolving the economic and political prob-lems of their own country" (Bresheeth, *Gulf and World Order*, 115). While the first statement reflects a departure from the previous regime, the second recalls Bourguiba's focus on national unity and internal affairs. The relationship between official and popular responses in Tunisia included overt cooperation, tacit agreement, and open confrontation.[7] The government's attitude was, however, mostly marked by controlled toler-ance of popular reaction. Yet the relaxation of state control, limited as it was, facilitated the free expression of popular sentiment in the street as well as in the press.

Cultural Representations of the Conflict

For Tunisians, the Gulf War was not a war *in* the Gulf; it was a domestic issue, indeed, the dominant concern. A long-repressed critical urge against both the West and certain Arab states was unleashed. And nowhere was it more present than in the press.[8] Events in the Gulf were practically the only subject of cultural production during the conflict. Newspapers opened their columns to writers and readers. *Al-Shurūq* maintained a regular page called *Adab al-'Irāq* (Literature about Iraq). It published poetry in colloquial and in standard Arabic and letters by volunteers to the war (24-1, 1991, pp. 12–13). There was even an imitation (*mu'āraḍa*) of a famous classical poem (*qasīda*) by al-Mutanabbī devoted to Saddām Ḥusayn (*al-Shurūq* 8 February 1991). There was also poetry in French in praise of Iraq and its leader (*Réalités* 1–7 February 1991).[9] The desire to put to rest a series of defeats that kept the Arab peoples, as a collective, at the margins of global history, was once again reemerging. Salīm Dawlat, writing in *al-Sha'b* (The People), the voice of organized labor in the country (U.G.T.T.), saw the "historical destiny" of Arabs at stake: "Hegel, the great German, said of Napoleon Bonaparte: 'This is history on horseback.' There is no reason why we should not say about Saddām Ḥusayn and the Iraqi people together—emulating this phrase in form and in spirit (despite the adaptation)—'This is history riding the future'" (*al-Sha'b* 25 January 1991). Despite the fact that Arab states were split on both sides of the confrontation, which made the war inter-Arab in some respect, in Tunisia the 1991 Gulf conflict was widely perceived as a Western war against Arabs. It reawakened old hopes and renewed a feeling of unity of destiny particularly at the level of popular sentiment. For reasons addressed later in the essay, cartoons were particularly effective in registering the pulse of society during the seven months of the crisis. They depicted the hopes, the apprehension, and the disillusionment of Tunisians during the conflict.[10] In the process, cartoons themselves would change in scope and gain more prominence. It was common to see an eight-year-old proudly displaying a drawing of Saddām Ḥusayn's serene face and formidable weaponry, instead of sports figures and American cartoon characters, on jeans or T-shirts. Traditional cartoon heroes had given way to the fascination with the warrior of the moment. Such a degree of politicization, however, has not always been the mark of Tunisian cartoons.

Cartoons in Tunisia

It was in emulation of French cartoons and in resistance to colonial French culture that the cartoon, as we know it today, was introduced into Tunisian press. Cartoons were an addition to a culture that had its own forms of oral and written humor such as *maqāma* and satirical poetry. ʿAll al-Dūʾājī (1909–49), the most prolific writer of his day—he was an accomplished short story writer, a cartoonist, playwright and song-writer—understood humor *(hazl* or *fukāha)* as an integral part of Arabic cultural heritage. He accused the contemporary press of aristocratic and smug attitudes towards art and set out to support the working people through his one-man newspaper *al-Surūr* (Happiness) (1936). Al-Dūʾājī writes: "People work hard: the worker in his factory and the farmer in his land. *Al-Surūr* entertains them and uplifts their spirit" (Dūʾājī, *tahta al-Sūr*, 58). Humoristic press was directed against colonial occupation, local impotent governors, and certain social customs. In the 1930s in particu-lar, there was a dramatic surge in political humor as a journalistic, liter-ary, and artistic style. ʿAlī al-Dūʾājī, al-Hadī al-ʿAbīdī, Ḥusayn al-Jazīrī, Ḥatim al-Makkī, ʿUmar al-Gharaʾirī and others led the effort in establish-ing humor as a viable style and as an artistic pursuit. There were unprece-dented successful attempts to devote entire newspapers to humor. *Al-Sardūk* (The Rooster), *al-Surūr* (Happiness), *al-Farzazzu* (The Beatle), *Juḥa* (Goha), *Jaḥjūḥ*, and others were widely circulated during the first half of the twentieth century.[11] More than thirty humor newspapers in Arabic alone had appeared in Tunisia before 1956. There were others in Hebrew, French and Italian. This genre of press had all but disappeared by the end of the 1950s. Today, only the independent French-language weekly *Tunis Hébdo* can be considered a systematic, although limited, effort to carry on what was a vibrant tradition.

As if the serious business of nation-state building precluded playful-ness, Tunisia's independence from direct French rule in 1956 witnessed a visible regression in humor in general, and in political caricature in particular. A similar trend took place in literature as well in the 1950s and 60s. The focus on depressed and depressing social conditions was reflected in the predominance of social realistic fiction and poetry. An attempt to fill the vacuum in the cartoon scene was led by the official daily *al-'Amal* (now *al-Ḥurriyya*), which hired 'Alī 'Abīd in 1966 as a professional cartoonist and began publishing daily caricatures on its last page. 'Abīd's career is at the center of cartooning in post-colonial Tunisia. He is a self-taught artist who credits his job as bodyguard for the former president Ḥabīb Būrgība (Bourguiba) with his interest in the caricature of foreign affairs: "Being in the Presidential Palace helped me a lot since I was able to observe political figures closely" (*al-Ṣaḥāfa* 11 July 1992).[12] He explains the decline of cartoon by lack of talented artists and the prevailing perception that caricature is a "minor art." 'Abīd sees his role as "double: artistic and journalistic."[13] He tends to draw without using speech balloons or verbal commentary: "In my drawings, I look for the elegance of line, drawing with the minimum possible in order to condense a large event into a small picture that can sometimes stand for a book" (*al-Ṣaḥāfa* 11 July 1992). His reliance on icons and internationally recognizable symbols made 'Abīd's work less culture-specific than that of most other cartoonists and allowed him to devote most of his talent to foreign affairs and prominent local cultural and sports events.[14] 'Abīd and other Tunisian cartoonists have, in fact, consistently refrained from the caricatural representation of local politicians or politics. Is this the result of state control or due to self-censorship?

In a personal interview, 'Abīd throws blame on prevailing social attitudes towards caricature. He notes that caricatural portrayal of officials is not forbidden by law but hampered by personal awareness as people continue to view cartoons as a *mahzala* or *huz'*, mockery or ridicule, not as an entertaining humorous representation or a constructive criticism.[15] Yet, it is common practice, in tightly ruled societies, to discourage any caricature of authority. Caricature is often perceived as a critical response to authority; not mere laughter, or inconsequential humor, but an inherently transgressive, if not subversive, gesture. Caricature, by definition, operates through the re-presentation of its cultural material in a "distorted" way. It is not an imitation of reality but a parodic and ironic representation. Yet, cartoons are deeply realistic. They transgress serious discourse by introducing what Mikhail Bakhtin, speaking of literature, calls the "corrective of laughter."[16] As cultural representations, cartoons are deeply intertextual, and, like most humor, very local. Because they are based on quick effect and condensation, they naturally draw on formulas, euphemisms, proverbs, and even clichés. In a culture that not only keeps alive its wide repertoire of popular sayings, but constantly invents new ones, Tunisian cartoonists seem to be well tuned in. Their verbal captions and commentary, as narrative, assume an implied reader (receiver) native to the culture and aware of its intimate (verbal) detail. Without knowledge of the soccer lingo, local proverbs, and the latest turns of phrase, the effect is likely to be lost and with it the whole effectiveness of the caricature.[17]

Cartoons During the Gulf Crisis

Throughout the 1980s comic strips, which had become a regular feature in several newspapers in Tunisia, were devoted to sports, social issues, and current events. The Gulf War would bring about a major change in focus and scope in cartoons. The subject of caricature would no longer be local society and culture but the Gulf War and its politics. Since information about the war originated almost exclusively in the tightly controlled Western media, cartoons (and to a lesser degree editorials) provided the commentary and the perspective about both the war and the Western media coverage of it.[18] Cartoons were particularly suited for such a role. Yet, one particular kind of cartoon was able to adapt to the rapid pace of the conflict more than others. The cartoonists of the newspapers *Tunis Hébdo*, *al-Akhbār* and *al-Shurūq*, who rely mostly on verbal commentary and quick line drawing, were able to capture the immediacy of events while providing their own critical edge. Other cartoonists, such as ʿAlī ʿAbīd, for instance, keen to preserve the elegance and density of their polished work, were less able (or less willing) to adapt.

A prominent instance of such adaptation can be observed in *Taʿsila kurawiyya* (Soccer Break or Nap), a comic strip devoted to soccer and conceived by Tawfīq al-Kūkī and published in the weekly independent *al-Akhbār*. It uses speech balloons in the Tunisian dialect and is therefore closed to readers unfamiliar with the idiom, the teams, and the players. During the war the strip became *ta'sīla khalījiyya* (Gulf Break). In the following strip there are four separate frames (fig. 1):

Following the same line, the strip "*Sérieux s'abstenir*" published in *Tunis Hébdo* is now framed with the missiles al-Husayn and al-'Abbas, barbed wire and explosives. The following strip links current soccer issues to the war (fig. 2):

In *Tunis Hébdo* as well, the weekly comic strip *Hébdrolmadaire* (Weekly comics or funnies), a collaboration between several artists, became *Hébdrolmaguerre* (Weekly war comics or funnies) as it was tak-

Figure 1

Frame 1: Ḥusayn: "You call yourself a man? Why don't you play face to face? Bush: "Cut this question! Don't put it on television!"

Frame 2: Ḥusayn: "The first game was at our home field. Wait for the one on yours!

Frame 3: Shamir: "Help!"
Bush: "What did you say?"

Frame 4: An Iraqi soldier with an eagle on one moustache and an Egyptian rooster on the other.
The soldier: "My only wish is to come face to face with Rambo".

(*al-Akhbār* 26 January 1991)

Figure 2

Frame 1: "Gulf War: The Tunisian Soccer Cup goes overboard once more."
Cup: "It is always me that gets sacrificed. I insist on self-determination" (allusion to the government's decision to postpone the Cup tournament for security reasons.)

Frame 2: Player from the team E.S.T. : "They did not want to have the games on Wednesday for fear of low returns. Well, the *huis-clos* (closed doors) served us well." (Games are normally played on Sunday; reference to the government's decision not to allow spectators into soccer games citing security reasons.)

Frame 3: A Soccer coach discusses strategy.
Reporter: "Are you still applying the defensive strategy 5-4-1?"
Coach : "No, sir. I am relying on the strategy of surprise by employing the new tactic . . . 'KHAFJI.'" (The allusion is to the Iraqi surprise attack on the Saudi town Ras al-Khafji.)

(*Tunis Hébdo* 25 February 1991)[19]

en over by the events of the war. Cartoons did not only change in focus. They increased in number and in scope as well. *Al-Akhbār*, for instance, published no less than six drawings in one of its issues (no. 354), *Tunis Hébdo* moved to two regular strips in addition to comic illustrations of its feature articles. Two areas captured the imagination of cartoonists and succeeded in becoming dominant motifs both during and after the war. These are media and technology.

Caricatures of the Media

Tunisian cartoons reveal awareness of two facets of the media. They show, on the one hand, a widespread belief that Western media, which had been until then highly regarded as an accurate and reliable source of information, had become discredited. C.N.N. epitomized this double status. While being watched through an increasing number of satellite dishes and quoted as an authoritative source of information about the war, it was often depicted as either the victim of censorship or in cahoots with the Pentagon. On the other hand, cartoons reveal a sense that local media resources had to be mobilized to counter the "distorted" reporting of the war. There was even a rare instance of trust in local official media, especially in television and radio. Distrust of Western media pointed to distrust of the West as a whole and reflected a growing awareness, as the crisis escalated into war, that local control on information by an independent media was an integral part of national independence and freedom. Both of these stances were reflected in cartoons.

Western media was subjected to relentless caricature. The cartoon "A Journalist with the Coalition" depicts a reporter wearing a gas mask "during the alert" and gagged with tape "after the alert" (fig. 3). He is unable, in either case, to speak up. (*Tunis Hébdo* 21–27 January 1991) In another drawing, a group of reporters receives news from a heavily guarded tank labeled "Western Media" (fig. 4). The cannon, in the shape of a loud speaker, announces: "*qatīl wāhid wa ... s.n.n... tsr.*" This may be read as, "One dead and... C.N.N. insists." By speaking from under the umbrella (literally under the tent) of Western forces, C.N.N. legitimizes the Coalition's claims and originates them at the same time. The Arabic com-

Figure 3

Figure 4

ment may also be read, *qatīl wāḥid wa ... sanantaṣir* (One dead and... we will win). C.N.N., in this case, blatantly speaks for and expresses the wishes of the coalition forces (*al-Ḥurriya* 2 March 1991).

In the face of one-sided reporting, there was a conscious effort to use media (and cartoons) to awaken public opinion. In one drawing, the sleeping public (viewer) is shaken up by an arm coming out of a television screen (*al-Shurūq* 18 February 1991). It reads "*Iṣḥa*" (Wake up!). This was a dramatic reversal in the role of media, especially official institutions routinely criticized for diverting citizens from serious issues and "drugging" them with lengthy superficial soap operas. During the war, the media acquired a new mission. It became an active agent in mobilizing disinterested citizens. A cartoon published in *Tunis Hébdo* gives the official local T.V. a "thumbs up!" (*Tunis Hébdo* 21-7 January 1991). The realization that this was a "media war," a conflict where media were used to influence the events directly, prompted cartoonists to turn it into a war against Western media.[20]

Technology and *"Technologie arabe"*

The Scud missile was perceived as a symbol of Iraqi inventiveness, power and courage. It was perhaps the Iraqi leader's sole lasting legacy and most effective asset even during the postwar period. Indeed, few things galvanized the public in Tunisia more than Saddām Ḥusayn's suc-

Figure 5

Figure 6

cess in penetrating the legendary shield of the Israeli air defense. The fact that Scud attacks on Israel and Saudi Arabia (42 and 46 attacks, respectively) were sudden and spaced out in time contributed to an unfolding narrative of the war full of elements of suspense and surprise. It is not surprising, therefore, that the Scud missiles al-Ḥusayn and al-ʿAbbās dominated the war cartoons both in quantity and in imaginative interpretations. There were numerous depictions of the Iraqi Scuds as male figures facing feminized American Patriot missiles. In one drawing, a Scud bearing the name "al-Husayn" whistles away heading to his target, unimpressed by the charm of a Patriot dressed to seduce (fig. 5). The cartoon reads "In order to make them (Patriots) more effective" (*Tunis Hébdo* 28 January 1991). In another, titled "The Corrida Continues," a bull fight takes place between a Patriot and a Scud missile (fig. 6). The Iraqi weapon swerves away elegantly, causing the Patriot to dash into the open air, angry and

Figure 7

Figure 8

defeated (*Tunis Hébdo* 18 February, 1991).

The United Nations sanctions were seen primarily as an American attempt to destroy Iraqi ballistic capabilities. A cartoon by ʿAbīd portrays George Bush riding a jet on its way to implement the U.N. resolutions as his declared goal, while his secret mission, inscribed in the back of the jet, is to destroy Iraqi Scuds (fig. 7). The action is conducted with the blessing and for the benefit of Israel, symbolized, as is conventional in these cartoons, by the Star of David (*al-Ḥurriya* 24 January 1991). In another drawing, Saddām Ḥusayn uses a Scud missile to squeeze Bush into linking the Gulf War to the Palestinian issue (fig. 8) (*al-Ḥurriya* 22 January 1991). The reference is to the Iraqi president's attempt to establish a direct link between the two issues and to drag Israel into the war, as he threatened to do early on in the conflict.[21]

When the war ended, Scuds turned into symbols of more mundane concerns, such as the ballistic (astronomical) rise of fish prices during Ramaḍān. One drawing depicts a Scud emerging from a fish pile heading towards a stunned customer (*al-Akhbār* 23 March 1991). An illustration for an article on the possible negative effects of the war on tourism in Tunisia shows a Western tourist on her way to the beach carrying a souvenir bag featuring the al-Husayn missile—memento from a war that is now hovering above the interests of an economy dependent on Western tourists (fig. 9) (*Tunis Hébdo,* n.d.).

Gulf War symbols have entered everyday idiom. Is it a nostalgic gesture, the "corrective of humor," or simply the nature of caricature where

Figure 9

everything, including a deadly war, is the stuff for a good laugh, for a "laughter break"? After the war, and in a constant displacement of symbols, the marketplace is politicized while the Scud missile loses its primarily political role.

Yet, despite such creative celebrations of the Scud, cartoons depicted signs of a clear and sobering realization that, in such a heavily technological war, Iraq had fallen short.[22] The "legendary" Iraqi ballistic weapon has fallen silent. In the strip *Hédrolmadaire technologie* devoted to poking fun at a presumed Arab technological "progress," the missile is now called "*skūt,*" meaning "silence," in a wicked pun on *skūd*, the Arabic for Scud (fig. 10). The drawing titled "EinCHICHAtein" depicts Einstein in traditional Tunisian attire smoking his water pipe (called *shīsha* in Tunisia, hence the pun). In another frame, two people in Gulf area dress attempt to blow each other up using locally manufactured bombs, as a *skūt* missile flies by. In a third frame, an Arab from the Gulf is pictured inside the belly of an American soldier with the comment: "Not only Iraqis have bankers, the opposite is true as well." On the subject of chemical weapons, the frame titled "Conventional weapons are available to everyone" portrays a man eating *Lablābī*, a Tunisian winter dish made with chick peas, a spicy broth, and bread crumbs, intoxicating a group of people with his gas. In another drawing, Shamir counts missiles (for sheep) to get sleep. This bitter and violent attack comes with a disclaimer:

Figure 10

"This *Hébdrolmadaire* is not directed against Iraq. It is directed at Arabs who will recognize themselves. For us, Iraq has emerged victorious from this war. We pay homage to the courage, heroism and vigilance of the Iraqi people."

Conclusion

In its 25 March 1991 issue, *Tunis Hébdo* published an intriguing and quite ambiguous cartoon that captures the meaning of the war. In the drawing, which plays on the local version of "Candid Camera" called "*al-Kāmira al-khafiyya*" (Hidden Camera), Saddām Ḥusayn's loss is depicted as a mere bad joke (fig. 11). A happy American extends his hand to a badly embattled Saddām Ḥusayn saying: "Thank you for your courage. It was 'Hidden Camera'." What to make of this caricature? Does it deny that the war took place? Certainly, Saddām Ḥusayn's wounds and bandages, the corpses and the burning buildings in the background of the

Figure 11

picture confirm the event. Yet, there is a clear sense that the whole war was a stage production. Does the cartoonist simply have in mind the poor taste and considerable harassment often used in the local television program "*al-Kāmira al-khafiyya*" (Hidden Camera)? It is true that immediately after the war the medium of cartoons quietly regained its familiar grounds: sports, Ramaḍān commentaries, and caricatures of Tunisians in their daily lives. *Al-Shurūq*, for instance, resumed its strip "Soccer

Break." Other newspapers did the same, most likely to cover their embarrassment and not to alienate a disappointed readership. The Gulf War seemed to recede in space, to become a conflict *in* the Gulf. Yet, besides the acute awareness that this war was made to *look* like a media event, that it was carried out as such, the cartoon "Hidden Camera" points up the sense that the war was real *only for* the embattled Iraq and its leader. The orchestration of the event effectively made the victim a guest on a T.V. program. Since he has no power to even prove, let alone convince, the spectators, of his victimization, his only choice is to laugh at his own impotence.

Did the war take place? Is this the meaning of Baudrillard's comment in the aftermath of the conflict, "The scandal today is no longer in the assault on moral values but in the assault on the reality principle"?[23] More than mere happening, the Gulf War was a time of general mobilization with few parallels in recent history. Its effects on Tunisia were immediate and pervasive. It impacted the way the government and the people related and changed the focus of local culture. Yet, for Tunisian cartoonists, just as for the most influential Arab cartoonist Nājī al-ʿAlī during the 1982 Israeli siege and subsequent occupation of Beirut, there was nothing more to say. It was a time of bitter disappointment and loss of a sense of direction. Arabs were once again teased into re-placing themselves in history. The difference is that now they can *see* their fate on the screen: abused guests on a program staged elsewhere and filmed through a hidden camera. The cartoonist, aware of the whole game, realizes that the global dynamics remains such that, this time around as well, history has repeated itself as a bad joke, as a farce.[24]

Notes

1. See in particular David Seddon,"Politics and the Gulf War Crisis: Government and Popular Responses in the Maghreb," in *The Gulf War and the New World Order*, ed. Haim Bresheeth and Nira Yuval-Davis (London: Zed Books ltd., 1991): 104–116. Walid Khalidi, however, reads the support for Saddam Hussein as "an index of the abysmal depth of disillusionment with the Arab status quo—political, social, and economic—as well as with the regional policies of the United States" ("Why Some Arabs Support

Saddam," in *The Gulf War Reader: History, Documents, Opinions* [New York: Times Books, 1991], 167.

2. Prime Minister, Zin al-Abidin Ben Ali, removed President Habib Bourguiba from office on November 7, 1987, just less than three years before the Gulf crisis.

3. When the war began, "the national assembly published a statement denouncing the attack on Iraq and expressing its solidarity with the Iraqi people in their resistance against 'the forces of destruction.' President Ben Ali, in a speech to the nation, appealed to Arab and Muslim leaders to put pressure on the U.N. Security Council for an end to the war in the Gulf and the calling of an international peace conference" (Bresheeth, *Gulf and World Order*, 108). The Tunisian official position had surprised and even angered the leader of the American-led coalition who, incidentally, did not forget or forgive such dissent. Tunisia quickly lost most of its American aid: "State Department officials confirmed that some US$30 million in military aid was to be withdrawn and economic aid cut from US $12.5 million to US $3 million" (ibid., 114). The reasons given are an increase in support for Egypt, Israel, and "'supportive' states like Morocco" (ibid.).

4. Yahia Zoubir, "Reactions in the Maghreb to the Gulf Crisis and War," in *Arab Studies Quarterly* 15, no.1 (Winter 1993): 83–103 (87) and Harry G. Summers Jr., ed., *Persian Gulf War Almanac* (New York: Facts on File, 1995), 63.

5. "The crisis in the Gulf generated in the Maghreb a popular mobilization in favor of Iraq far greater than anywhere else in the Arab and Muslim world with the exception, perhaps, of Jordan and the occupied territories" (Zoubir, 93).

6. The campaign to gather material support for Iraq had to close early because of lack of storage space (Bresheeth, *Gulf and World Order*, 110).

7. Zoubir takes note of these varying postures in his well-documented essay "Reactions in the Maghreb to the Gulf Crisis and War": "The Ben Ali regime itself, unlike Habib Bourguiba's during the Arab-Israeli wars, adopted an attitude more in line with the popular mood" (Zoubir, "Reactions," 93). And he adds: "Tunisian government, fearful of *dépassement* (spill-overs, excesses), tried unsuccessfully to forbid public demonstrations in the capital" (Ibid., 95).

8. Research in Tunisia was undertaken in the summer of 1992. Unless otherwise noted, all translations are my own. This piece is dedicated to Achraf Omri.

9. Prominent Tunisian writers published scathing attacks against Arab intellectuals who did not lend full support to Iraq. Two such pieces were direct-

ed against Naguib Mahfuz; one appeared in *al-Shurūq* (15 February 1991) and the other in *al-Akhbār* (9 February 1991).

10. The Tunisian sociologist Mahmūd al-Dhawwādī, faced with the over-whelming and for him unexplainable public euphoria, suggested that "the social contract during the war was dominated by irrational thinking," such as belief in the supernatural powers of Saddām Ḥusayn. According to him, the popular disappointment that followed the war was the direct outcome of "irrational expectations" (*Réalités* 28 March 1991). Stories of the supernat-ural and prophetic accounts which circulated in Tunisia during the war are subject to a narratological study by Faraj Ibn Ramaḍān. "'*Ajā'ib al-akhbār fī ayyām ḥarb al-khalīj*" (Unusual Stories During the Gulf War), in *al-Qiṭā al-hāmishī fī al-sard al-ʿarabī* (Tunis: Dār al-Bīrūnī li al-nashr, n.d.): 15–51.

11. See *Dalīl al-Dawriyyāt al-Ṣādira bi Tūnis, 1838–1956* (Guide to Periodicals Published in Tunisia, 1838–20 March 1956) (Carthage: Bayt al-ḥikma, 1989) for statistics, dates and full entries of individual publications.

12. ʿAlī ʿAbīd, interview by Sāsī Jbīl, *al-Ṣaḥāfa* 11 July 1992.

13. ʿAlī ʿAbīd, interview by the author, tape recording, Tunis, Tunisia, 9 July 1992.

14. See *Caricatures de Aly Abid* (Tunis: A.G.E.P., 1976) for a representative collection of ʿAbīd's drawings in the 1960s and 70s.

15. Abīd, interview by the author, 9 July 1992.

16. Bakhtin writes in "From the Pre-history of Novelistic Discourse": "Parodic-travestying literature introduces the permanent corrective of laughter, of a critique on the one-sided seriousness of the lofty direct word, the corrective of reality that is always richer, more fundamental and most importantly too contradictory and heteroglot to be fit into a high and straightforward genre" (*The Dialogic Imagination,* trans. Caryl Emerson and Michael Holquist [Austin: University of Texas Press, 1981], 55.

17. In a drawing where a Scud missile tears through Yitzhak Shamir's eye, we read: "*Skūd fī ʿīn laḥsūd*" (Scud in the eye of the envious). The Tunisian read-er will immediately pick up on the reference to the saying "*Ud fī ʿīn laḥsūd*" (Break a stick in the eye of the envious) (*al-Akhbār* 26 January 1991). The pun adds immediacy and effectiveness to the message that Israel is envious of Iraqi military achievements.

18. One facet of the control of information the U.S.-led coalition had so effec-tively exercised during the crisis had to do with restricting coverage, and at times completely ignoring opposition to the war around the world. *The Triumph of Image: The Media's War in the Gulf—a Global Perspective,* ed. Hamid Mawlana, George Gerbner, Herbert T. Schiller (Boulder: Westview

Press, 1992) documents and analyses the negative reaction to Western intervention in the Gulf in India, Japan, Malaysia, Jordan, Egypt, and other countries. Although there is no systematic study of reaction in North Africa in the book, the following comment offers a glimpse into the reporting of what was happening there: "Five-second flashes of huge rallies held in North African cities against the war were completely inadequate in providing a sense of the massive opposition in that part of the world to American policy" (Mawlana, *Triumph*, 26).

19. The attack took place on January 29, 1991. Al-Khafji remained under Iraqi control until February 2. For detail and a chronology of the war, see *Mawsū'at Ḥarb al-Khalīj* (Encyclopedia of the Gulf War), 2 vols., ed. Fu'ād Maṭar (Beirut: Al-Mu'assasa al-'arabiyya li al-dirāsāt wa al-nashr, 1994) and *Persian Gulf War Almanac* (1995).

20. See in particular the essays by Noam Chomsky and Andre Gunder Frank in the meticulous and wide-ranging study of media coverage of the Gulf War, *Triumph of the Image* (1992).

21. There is of course the memory of the Israeli attack on the Iraqi military facility in Tammuz in the early 80s as well.

22. The Moroccan intellectual Mahdī al-Manjara declares in an interview with the Tunisian newspaper *al-Baṭal* on 6 February 1991: "Il n'est pas permis a un pays du tiers-monde, et surtout s'il est arabe, d'aquérir une autonomie technologique" ("It is not permissible that a Third-world country, particularly if it is Arab, can acquire technological independence") (*Premīere guerre civilisationnelle* [Casablanca: Les editions Toubkal, 1992], 73).

23. Jean Baudrillard, *The Gulf War Did not Take Place*, trans. Paul Patton (Bloomington: Indiana Univ. Press, 1995), 76. The book is made up of three articles published in French before, during, and after the war with the titles: "The Gulf War Will not Take Place", "The Gulf War: Is it Really Taking Place?", and "The Gulf War Did not Take Place."

24. Karl Marx writes in "The Eighteenth Brumaire of Louis Bonaparte": "Hegel remarks somewhere that all facts and personages of great importance occur, as it were, twice. He forgot to add: the first time as tragedy, the second as farce" (Carl Marx and Frederick Engels, *Selected Writings* [New York: International Publishers, 1968], 96).

Works Cited

ʿAbīd, ʿAlī. *Caricatures de Aly Abid*. Tunis: A.G.E.P., 1976.

Al-ʿAbīdī, al-Hādī. *Taḥta al-sūr*. Tunis: ʿAbd al-Karīm Ibn ʿAbd al-Lāh, 1992.

Bakhtin, Mikhail. *The Dialogic Imagination*, trans. Caryl Emerson and Michael Holquist. Austin: University of Texas Press, 1981.

Baudrillard, Jean. *The Gulf War Did not Take Place,* trans. Paul Patton. Bloomington: Indiana Univ. Press, 1995.

Bresheeth, Haim, and Nira Yuval-Davis, eds. *The Gulf War and the New World Order*. London: Zed Books Ltd., 1991.

al-Dūʿājī, ʿAlī. *Taḥta al-sūr*, ed. ʿIzz al-Dīn al-Madanī. Tunis: al-dār al-tūnisiyya li al-nashr, n.d.

Ḥamdān, Muḥammad. *Dalīl al-dawriyyāt al-ṣādira bi Tūnis: 1838–1956* (Guide to Periodicals Published in Tunisia from 1838 until 20 March 1956). Carthage: Bayt al-ḥikma, 1989.

Ibn Ramaḍān, Faraj . "ʿA*jāib al-akhbār fī ayyām ḥarb al-khalīj*" (Unusual Stories During the Gulf War) in *al-QiṬaʿ al-hāmishī fī al-sard al-ʿarabī* (The Marginal Sector in Arabic Narrative). Tunis: Dār al-Bīrūnī li al-nashr, n.d. (15–51).

Al-Manjara (Elmandjara), Mahdi. *Premĩere guerre civilisationnelle*. Casablanca: Les editions Toubkal, 1992. Rabat: Dār Ṭubqal, 1992

Marx, Karl, and Frederick Engels. *Selected Writings*. New York: International Publishers, 1968.

Maṭar, Fuʾād, ed. *Mawsūʿat ḥarb al-khalīj* (Encyclopedia of the Gulf War), 2 vols. Beirut: Al-Muʾassasa al-ʿarabiyya li al-dirāsāt wa al-nashr, 1994.

Mawlana, Hamid, George Gerbner, and Herbert T. Schiller, eds. *Triumph of the Image: The Media's War in the Persian Gulf—a Global Perspective*. Boulder: Westview Press, 1992.

Sifry, Micah L., and Christopher Cerf, eds. *The Gulf War Reader: History, Documents, Opinions*. New York: Times Books, 1991.

Summers, Harry G., Jr., ed. *Persian Gulf War Almanac*. New York: Facts on File, 1995.

Zoubir, Yahia. "Reactions in the Maghreb to the Gulf Crisis and War." In *Arab Studies Quarterly* 15, no.1 (Winter 1993): 83–103.

Tunisian Newspapers

*al-Ṣaḥāfa (*Official government newspaper).

*al-Akhbār (*Independent weekly in Arabic)

al-Hurriya. (The official newspaper of the R.C.D., the ruling party in Tunisia)

al-Shaʿb. (Newspaper of the U.G.T.T, the main labor union.)

al-Shurūq. (Independent Daily)

Réalitées. (Independent bilingual weekly magazine.)

Tunis Hébdo. (Independent weekly in French.)

ʿAlī ʿAbīd. Interview with the author. Tape Recording. Tunis, Tunisia. 9 July 1992.

The Missing Piece.
The Place to Start.

Filled Marriage

VIDEO STUDY

Dr. Tim and Darcy Kimmel

family
matters
building grace-based relationships

GRACE FILLED MARRIAGE SERIES

GREATNESS

CHARACTER
FREEDOMS
INNER NEEDS